Indoor Gardener's Green Thumb Guide

by

Arnold and Connie Krochmal

DRAKE PUBLISHERS INC.

NEW YORK ● LONDON

Published in 1974 by
Drake Publishers Inc.
381 Park Avenue South
New York, N.Y. 10016

ISBN 87749-663-3

Printed in The United States of America

This book is dedicated with deep affection to Dr. T. B. Mitchell, Professor Emeritus of Entomology, North Carolina State University, Raleigh, known to the Class of '42 and other classes as "Rat" Mitchell.

Our recent three year assignment at North Carolina State was much enriched by the renewal of a thirty-five-year-old relationship, and the Thursday night buffets made much more savory by his company.

He is a glowing example of teacher, scholar and scientist, whose love of knowledge, concern for students and dedication to science wax brighter with each passing year.

"Ace Krochmal, Class of '42, N.C.S.U., Adjunct Professor, Botany N.C.S.U., Connie Krochmal

ACKNOWLEDGEMENTS

Writing this book has been truly a labor of love for us and if our readers and those who helped us enjoy reading the book as much as we did writing it, we will be content.

As in the past our friend Dr. I. T. Littleton, and his splendid staff at the D.H. Hill Library at North Carolina State University, provided every bit of support and help we could possibly have wished for, and more.

One of our favorite department stores, Hammacher Schlemmer in New York, kindly aided us time and time again with materials from their garden department for us to use in our studies. Our belief that New Yorkers are among the friendliest of peoples was greatly strengthened.

Our photographs and illustrations came from many places. Ms. Mary Cowell, Photo Librarian of the United States Department of Agriculture; Charles Balducci; the Agricultural Extension Services of Cornell University; Clemson and North Carolina State Universities; Pennsylvania State University; the Universities of Maryland, Connecticut, Minnesota and California at Berkeley; Polestar and Parker Seed Company; Professor Paul Smeal, Virginia Polytechnic Institute; Longwood Gardens, Kennett Square, Pennsylvania, all answered our requests graciously and promptly.

Ideal Toy Company, Comspec and Asgrow Seed Company helped when needed.

A special note of thanks to Dr. Fred Cochrane, Horticulture Department, North Carolina State University, who offered both encouragement and assistance.

CONTENTS

Chapter 1

APARTMENT GARDENING

City dwellers with limited opportunities to walk in the fields and woods, can, on a small scale, bring part of the plant world into their homes. Even a compact efficiency apartment can be a home for a number of friendly, living, breathing green plants.

Requiring a minimum of attention, no veterinary care, no walking and being both quiet and clean, plants are ideal city pets. They do not require daily feeding, and self-watering devices may be bought which make it possible to leave plants alone for days and weeks at a time.

Whatever light exposures an apartment or house may have, there is a living green plant that will flourish. Even in apartments with no light, a simple and inexpensive electric light and timer will supply plants with the energy they need to be happy and do their best to please you with healthy leaves and handsome flowers and fruits.

House plants, whether climbing, hanging or resting quietly in some tranquil part of the room, improve the appearance of their surroundings as no other object can. When cared for properly, house plants can and do thrive for many years. We know of families that pass on plants and cuttings from generation to generation, much as a treasured heirloom. Each bloom is an occasion for nostalgic remembrances of times past. Dr. Nannette Henderson, who wrote the chapter on plant diseases, has a plant that has been in her family for nearly a hundred years. This is one heirloom that can be divided to provide each family member with an equally fine plant. A few cuttings propagated from time to time will suffice to keep all descendants and rela-

1

tives happy, with families intact and speaking to one another. As families grow, new cuttings can be taken and passed on to plant-loving members. If a thriving specimen is lost due to fire, disease, floods or tornadoes, it can easily be replaced with little expense and no heartaches.

Home gardening offers an opportunity for a creative outlet in a small area and at little cost. Miniature gardens in plates, and terrariums in aquariums, as well as in pint and quart jars, can duplicate a desert scene, a swamp, the forest floor or a formal Japanese garden. Tomatoes, chives, and other herbs can all be grown indoors.

Once people thought plants removed oxygen from the air. Actually, plants remove carbon dioxide from the air and add oxygen in small amounts during the day. At night the process is reversed, but the amounts of carbon dioxide that are released are too small to be of any concern.

Growing plants in a home presents some challenges but by proper selection of plants, by knowing the growth requirements of the plants, and by adjusting the environment within the recommended limits of light, temperature and humidity, the problems can be overcome.

Ventilation

Natural gas, if pure, is not harmful to plants, but if it is mixed with artificial gas it can cause injury and death to plants.

Butane, propane and ethane gas are not harmful in trace amounts. Gas leaking from a defective oven or from too long a delay in lighting a gas stove can be injurious to plants. Faulty coal furnaces and improperly operating kerosene heaters can also cause injury.

Temperature

A night temperature drop of more than 10 degrees from a day range of 65-75°F. can be damaging to many plants. Night temperatures as low as 50°F. can be tolerated by most flowering plants, with the exception of African violets and gloxinia. Most foliage plants prefer slightly warmer temperatures, about 80°F. during the day and 60-75°F. at night. Lower temperatures can be used if plants are gradually accustomed to cooler nights, and if the more sensitive are covered with plastic bags each night.

For plants on or near our window sills we close the curtains at night when the temperature goes down, and more sensitive plants are moved into the room away from the windows, which are usually cold spots unless there are storm windows in place.

Never place plants in front of or above heat outlets in the cool season, or air conditioners during summer, as the blasts of air are harmful, increasing water loss and dehydration among other damages.

Plants recommended for offices

The temperature in offices varies, especially during the evening and on weekends. The light is usually poor and plants are often placed near drafty locations such as windows, doors and heat outlets, so offices do indeed require special plants that can withstand these conditions.

>aralia, *Polyscias* spp.
>Chinese evergreen, *Aglaonema modestum*
>dracaena, *Dracaena* spp.
>dumb cane, *Dieffenbachia* spp.
>fig, *Ficus benjamina* and *F. retusa nitida*
>jade plant, *Crassula* spp.
>Norfolk Island pine, *Araucaria excelsa*
>philodendron, *Philodendron* spp.
>pothos, *Scindapsus aureus*
>spathiphylum, *Spathiphylum floribundum*
>ti plant, *Cordyline terminalis*

Chapter 2

LIGHT

This chapter is one of the most important in the book for adequate light is the absolutely indispensable factor in growing plants in the home.

Without sunlight, or an acceptable substitute, green plants cannot manufacture the food they need to grow and survive and they soon die.

If sunlight is low in intensity, or lacking, in a part of the home or office, a supplemental light source is required.

Different kinds of plants require varying amounts of light to grow well. In each chapter, for each class of house plants, we have given the *optimum* light requirements for each plant. These requirements are not strictly inflexible but will vary with room temperature, water and humidity and the age of the plants. Flowering plants, cacti and succulents generally require higher light quantities than do foliage plants.

To measure light we have used a very inexpensive light meter (Figure 1) that is useful in determining light in foot candles. The upper scale measures light in lux units when the knob at the lower right is set at x (Figure 1). Multiply the reading on the upper dial by 10 to give you foot candles, the common unit of measurement used for plants. This handy little meter also measures temperatures in F°. on the lower scale.

Table 1 provides a guide to the amount of light commonly found at different exposures under a range of conditions as measured at noon on a bright sunny day, by standing where the plant will be placed, and pointing the meter at the light source. Knowing the exposure you plan on using and the approximate available light means you can select plants adapted to that particular light situation, giving you a good start in successful home gardening.

If possible, consider rotating plants every week or so to provide light to all sides as an aid to uniform growth.

In summary we note that many plants will thrive in *direct sunlight,* including the artillery plant, cacti, Christmas cactus, geranium, kalanchoe, snake plant and stonecrop. South exposure, or east or west exposures receiving several hours of sunlight, are suitable for this class of plants.

Shade tolerant plants are usually foliage species grown for the beauty of their leaves. Included in this category are the dumb cane, Chinese evergreen, fiddleleaf fig, grape ivy, peperomia, philodendron, rubber plant and snake plant. All are well suited for northern exposure with poor, weak light.

Partial shade plants include flowering as well as foliage species such as African violet, Boston fern, caladium, Chinese

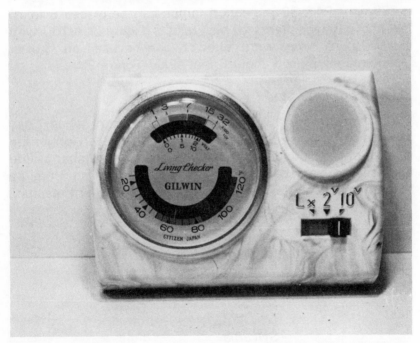

Figure 1. This light meter measures light in lux units when the knob at the lower right is set at x. Multiply the reading by 10 to get foot candles. The lower scale measures temperatures in F°. *A. Krochmal*

evergreen, croton, dracaena, dumb cane, grape ivy, peperomia and rubber plant, which need somewhat more light than
the shade tolerant plants.

SUNLIGHT SUBSTITUTES

Incandescent light

Electric light can be used partially or entirely to substitute
for sunlight. The equipment needed can range from a goose-
neck desk lamp with a 75-watt bulb to combinations of incandescent bulbs and fluorescent tubes.

Incandescent bulbs of the kind we all use at home, frosted
or clear, are satisfactory for growing plants indoors. They are
inexpensive and their color composition is very close to
sunlight, strong in blues and reds. Their biggest drawbacks is
the high amount of heat they generate and the irrelatively
short life span. They can be used with a reflector or in some
cases bought with a built-in reflector.

150-watt PAR-38 projection lamps can be placed 8 to 10
feet above foliage plants for best results (Figure 2). A 150-watt
incandescent lamp, with reflector, can be used on shorter
foliage plants, placed about 6 feet away (Figure 2).

Fluorescent light

Much in use are a wide variety of fluorescent tubes. They
produce more light with less heat and have a much longer life
span than the incandescent bulbs. There are a number of fine
fluorescent tubes available for indoor plant growing. Here, by
brand name, are a few we have used with excellent results:

General Electric
Daylight
Cool white
Plant light

Duro-Test
Vita-Lite

Sylvania
Gro-Lux
Wide spectrum Gro-Lux

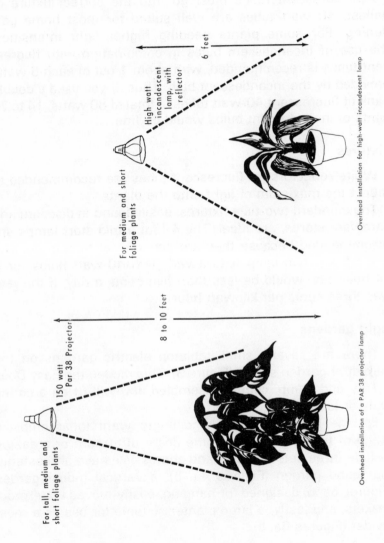

Figure 2. *(Left)* For foliage plants place a 150-watt PAR-38 projection lamp 8–10 feet away from the plant. *(Right)* For shorter foliage plants place this 150-watt incandescent bulb with reflector, 6 feet above the plant. *Cornell Extension Service.*

Westinghouse
Plant-Gro
Agrolite

All fluorescent tubes must go into the correct fixture or ballast, 40 watt tubes are well suited for most home gardening. For some plants needing higher light intensities, the use of incandescent bulbs in combination with fluorescent tubes is recommended, with about 1 out of each 5 watts provided by the incandescent bulb. Thus, if you used a double bank of fluorescent 40-watt tubes, a total of 80 watts, 14 to 20 watts of incandescent bulbs would be fine.

Fixtures

White reflectors for fluorescent tubes are recommended to reflect the maximum of light onto the plants.

The standard two-tube fixtures, easily found at discount and hardware stores, are ideal. The 4-foot, rapid-start lamps are recommended because they are economical to operate. The cost of one two-lamp fixture with two 40-watt bulbs for a 14-hour day, would be less than five cents a day, if the rate was three cents per kilowatt hour.

Light gardens

There are several small tabletop electric gardens on the market at garden stores (Figure 3). This model, the Easy Does It Tray and Lamp, comes assembled and will fit on a coffee table or tabletop.

For the home gardener who might want to assemble a range of fixtures to go with the decor of a room or area, we include three sets of plants and photos. We have a freestanding round garden (Figures 4a, b), a vertical indoor garden (Figures 5a, b) designed for hanging, easily-moved waterproof baskets, and lastly, a large planter suitable for use as a room divider (Figures 6a, b).

Vacation lights

When we go on vacation we prefer to leave our plants in subdued light, usually out of direct sunlight. We can create our idea of ideal light by drawing our sheer curtains. However, if we plan on being gone at a time when we feel some light supplement is needed we use a timing device (Figure 7) that turns the lights on at a pre-selected time and turns them off at a pre-selected time. If you are using incandescent bulbs be sure they are not too close to the plant as they can cause burning.

We use incandescent bulbs during the winter, timed to go on at night and off early in the morning, as a protection against unexpected night temperature drops.

Table 1: Light ratings of various exposures at midday of a bright, sunny day.

Low Light 50- to 150-foot candles

North window exposure

In front of the window with most of the sky blocked.

3 to 5 feet back from, or on either side, with a clear view of the sky.

Figure 3. An Easy Does It Tray and Lamp that comes assembled and ready to set on your tabletop. *Parker Seed Co.*

Figures 4a and b. This lovely free-standing round light garden is decorative in addition to providing the plant with light. *U.S.-D.A.*

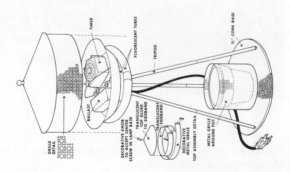

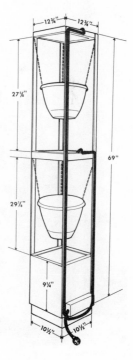

Figures 5a and b. A vertical indoor planter with sleek, uncluttered lines designed for hanging baskets. *U.S.D.A.*

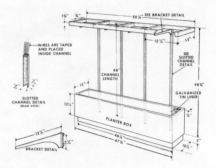

Figure 6a and b. This large attractive planter which will hold taller plants can be used as a room divider. *U.S.D.A.*

East or west window exposures

3 to 5 feet back from the window with most of the sky blocked.

6 to 10 feet back from the window with a clear view of the sky.

South window exposures

Up to 10 feet back from, or 3 to 5 feet on either side of, the window with most of the sky blocked.

Up to 15 or 20 feet back from, or 5 to 8 feet on either side of, the window with a clear view of the sky.

Medium Light 150- to 200-foot candles

North window exposure

Directly in front of the window with a clear view of the sky.

Figure 7. Timers that can be used to turn lights off and on during your absence. *A. Krochmal*

East or west window exposure

Directly in front of the window with about half of the sky blocked from view.

3 to 5 feet from, or just to either side of, the window with a clear view of the sky.

South window exposure

Up to 10 feet back from, or 2 to 3 feet on either side of, the window with a clear view of the sky.

High Light 200- to 450-foot candles

East or west window exposure

Directly in front of the window with a clear view of the sky.

South window exposure

Directly in front of the window with about half of the sky blocked from view.

Up to 5 feet back from, or just to either side of, with a clear view of the sky.

Direct Light 1000- to 1500-foot candles

This would be a category providing direct sunlight unimpeded by curtains or barriers, usually a south window exposure.

REQUIREMENTS FOR SELECTED HOUSE PLANTS

Temperature

cool = 40-60°F.
medium = 60-65°F.
warm = above 65°F.

Watering

Dry—These should dry out between waterings and need watering only every 1½–2 weeks. If watered too often the plants will probably lose their leaves and the roots may rot.

Medium—These need watering every 3–7 days. These plants will also be damaged if allowed to dry out. Do not water too often since this would cause too rapid growth as well as possible damage to the plant.

Moist—Water every other day. These would be damaged if allowed to dry out. They are not kept moist to the touch but rather are kept to the same degree of moistness at all times.

Low Light

Plant	Water	Temperature	Mature Plant Size
ferns	moist	warm	pot, floor
gold dust plant, Aucuba japonica "variegata"	moist	cool to medium	tree, floor plant
palms	moist	warm	pot, tree, floor
spindletree, Euonymus spp.	moist	medium	pot

Medium Light

Plant	Water	Temperature	Mature Plant Size
achimenes, Achimenes spp.	moist	medium	pot
caladium, Caladium bicolor	moist	warm	pot
calathea, Calathea spp.	moist	warm	pot
cape cowslip, Lachenalia spp.	medium	cool	pot
cape primrose, Streptocarpus spp.	moist	medium	pot
cast iron plant, Aspidistra lurida	medium	cool to medium	pot
Chinese evergreen, Aglaonema spp.	dry	warm	pot
cineraria, Senecio cruentus, and German ivy, Senecio mikanioides	moist	cool	pot
cissus, Cissus spp.	moist	medium	pot
columnea, Columnea spp.	moist	medium	pot
crossandra, Crossandra spp.	moist	warm	pot
dracaena, Dracaena spp.	dry to medium	medium	pot, floor
dumb cane, Dieffenbachia spp.	dry to medium	medium	pot, floor
dwarf boxwood, Buxus sempervirens	moist	medium	pot

	moisture	temperature	location
fat lizzie, *Fatshedera lizei*	moist	cool	pot
fig, *Ficus* spp.	moist	medium	floor, pot, tree
flame violet, *Episcia* spp.	moist *water everyother day*	warm 65+	pot
flamingo flower, *Anthurium* spp.	moist	medium	pot
fuchsia, *Fuchsia* spp.	moist	medium	pot
Japanese aralia, *Fatsia japonica*	moist	cool	floor, pot
nephtytis, *Syngonium podophyllum*	dry	warm	pot
peperomia, *Peperomia* spp.	medium	medium	pot
philodendron, Philodendron spp., some will tolerate less light	dry to medium	warm	tree, floor, pot
pilea, *Pilea* spp.	moist	medium	pot, floor
pothos, *Scindapsus aureus*	moist	medium to warm	pot
pouch flower, *Calceolaria* spp.	medium	cool	pot
purple waffle plant, *Hemigraphis exotica*	medium	medium	pot
seersucker plant, *Geogenanthus undatus*	moist	warm	pot
shamrock, *Oxalis* spp.	medium *water 3-7 days*	medium 60°-65°	pot
silvervein fittonia, *Fittonia verschaffelti argyroneura*	moist	warm	pot
snake plant, *Sansevieria* spp.	dry *between watering*	warm 65+	pot
spider aralia, *Dizygotheca elegantissima*	moist	warm	floor, pot
spider plant, *Chlorophytum capense*	moist *every other day*	warm 65+	pot
strawberry geranium, *Saxifraga sarmentosa*	medium 3-7 days	cool 40°-60°	pot
three men in a boat, *Rhoeo discolor*	moist *every other day*	medium 60-65°	pot
ti plant, *Coryline terminalis*	moist	medium	pot
Transvaal daisy, *Gerbera jamesoni*	medium	warm	pot
wax plant, *Hoya carnosa*	medium	medium	pot

High Light

Plant	Water	Temperature	Mature Plant Size
African violet, *Saintpaulia* spp.	moist	warm	pot
aphelandra, *Aphelandra* spp.	moist	warm	pot
aralia, *Polyscias* spp.	moist	warm	floor, pot
azalea, *Rhododendron* spp.	medium	cool	pot
baby tears, *Helxine soleiroli*	moist	cool	pot
beefstock plant, *Iresine* spp.	moist	cool to medium	pot
begonia, *Begonia* spp.	moist *every other day*	warm *65+*	pot
calla lily, *Zantedschia aethiopica*	moist	medium	pot
chocolate plant, *Pseudcranathemum alatum*	medium	medium	pot
Christmas cactus, *Zygocactus truncatus*	medium *3-7 days*	cool *48-60°*	pot
chrysanthemum, *Chrysanthemum* spp.	moist	medium to warm	pot
cyclamen, *Cyclamen* spp.	moist	cool	pot
Easter lily, *Lilium longiflorum*	moist	medium	pot
English ivy, *Hedera helix*	moist	cool	pot
fairy rose, *Rose chinensis minima*	moist	warm	pot
geranium, *Pelargonium* spp.	medium	cool	pot
gloxinia, *Sinningia speciosa*	moist	warm	pot
Japanese aralia, *Fatsia japonica*	moist	medium	floor, pot
Jerusalem cherry, *Solanum pseudo-capsicum*	moist	cool	pot
Kenilworth ivy, *Cymbalaria muralis*	moist	cool to medium	pot
lantana, *Lantana camara*	moist	warm	pot
marigold, *Calendula* spp.	dry to medium	cool to medium	pot

Plant	Moisture	Temperature	Container
mock orange, *Pittosporum tobira*	moist	cool	floor, pot
Norfolk Island pine, *Araucaria excelsa*	moist to medium	cool 48°-60°	tree, floor, pot
oleander, *Nerium oleander*	moist	medium	pot
ornamental pepper, *Capsicum frutescens*	medium	cool	pot
podocarpus, Podocarpus macrophylla	dry to medium	cool	floor, tree, pot
poinsetta, *Euphorbia pulcherrima*	medium 3-7	medium 60°-65°	pot
prayer plant, *Maranta spp.*	moist	warm 65+	pot
primrose, *Primula obconia, P. malacoides.*	medium	medium	pot
schefflera, *Schefflera actinophylla*	dry to medium	cool to medium	tree, floor, pot
screwpine, *Pandanus veitchi*	moist	warm	pot
spathiphylum, *Spathiphylum clevelandi*	moist	medium	pot
succulents and cactus	medium	warm	pot
velvet plant, *Gynura aurantiaca*	moist	medium 60°-65°	pot
wandering Jew, *Tradescantia fluminensis, and Zebrina pendula*	moist	warm 65+	pot

Direct Light

Plant	Moisture	Temperature	Container
amarylis, *Amarylis spp.*	moist	medium to warm	pot
calamondin orange, *Citrus mitis*	dry	warm	pot
citrus other than calamondin, *Citrus spp.*	moist	warm	floor, tree, pot
coleus, *Coleus spp.*	moist	cool 48°-60°	pot
croton, *Codiaeum variegatum*	moist	warm	pot
gardenia, *Gardenia spp.*	moist	medium	pot
hibiscus, *Hibiscus roseo-sinensis*	moist	warm	pot
impatiens, *Impatiens spp.*	moist	warm 65+	pot

Chapter 3

FEEDING AND WATERING

This chapter was probably the most difficult one in the book for us to write. Both fertilizing and watering are as much an art as a science. A sensitivity to the appearance of your plants and a knowledge of how they look when well fed and watered is really the basis of a fruitful program.

Fertilizer

A look at the fertilizer shelf in a garden shop can be startling. This morning we went over to a nearby garden center to pass a little time in pleasant surroundings. We were interested to see that there were several package fertilizers for roses. One was labelled 11–6–4, another 10–7–5 and a third 6–10–4. How in the world does one decide which to use? Which formula is best?

First, let us see what the formula, the three numbers, really mean.

Nitrogen-N

The first number is a percent figure for nitrogen (N). 10 means 10 percent, or 10 pounds of nitrogen per 100 pounds of fertilizer. Nitrogen is essential to vegetative growth, that is, the parts of the plant above ground. When N is deficient, plant growth is stunted and the foliage turns a pale yellow. However, too much nitrogen can push the plant into an extreme vegetative stage and reduce or totally inhibit flowering. Such plants are weak and very dark green.

In the broadest term more nitrogen is needed for young plants making their first growth and for plants beginning seasonal growth prior to flowering. Less nitrogen is needed as plants flower and then die back.

Phosphorus-P

The second number in the formula refers to the percentage of phosphorus. This nutrient is important to proper root growth, flowering and fruiting.

Too much phosphorus can increase flower production at the cost of a stunted plant. Too little phosphorus causes plants to be slow to flower and seed and fruits are dwarfed. Phosphorus is needed for best flowering. Some plants demonstrate a reddish-purple foliage color when phosphorus is deficient.

Potassium-K

The third number refers to potassium whose role is not quite so clear cut as the first two. One of the functions of potassium in a plant is to lessen the tendency to wilting due to water loss from the plant. K also plays a role in strengthening stems and is involved to some extent in providing resistance to insects and certain fungus diseases.

Feeding

If you use a good rich soil when potting you do not need any fertilizer for three or four months or until the plants have become established and the root system begins to grow! Do not fertilize dormant plants nor newly purchased plants in flower. Growing plants may need fertilizer every six to ten weeks.

By far the easiest way to fertilize potted plants is with the liquid form whether bought that way or mixed by you. If you use an already mixed liquid form, follow the directions. If you mix your own, select a low analysis fertilizer such as 5-10-5 or a 4-12-4. Dissolve a teaspoon in a quart of warm but not hot water, stir well and allow to stand overnight.

Apply the fertilizer solution during the growing period at intervals of six to ten weeks, applying enough each time to wet the soil thoroughly.

Low analysis dry fertilizers can be used, particularly if they are of the slow release type. But never, never apply liquid or dry fertilizer to dry soil or severe root damage may result.

Special comments

Acid loving plants such as azaleas, camellias and gardenias lose their bright green foliage color if the soil is too alkaline. This condition is called *chlorosis,* or lack of color. The problem can be handled by adding a small amount of cholated iron to the pot, or a little powdered sulfur once a year. The iron remedies the chlorosis and the sulfur remedies the cause, alkalinity.

As with our other house pets, dogs and cats, in house plants overeating is much more of a problem than undereating. Over-fertilizing can cause burned looking leaf margins, very heavy vegetative growth and in extreme cases, death.

Watering

Amounts

The plant's need for water will depend on its age, size, vigor, room temperature, light exposure and humidity in the air.

A successful plantsperson will quickly learn to read the condition of the plant and soil to know if watering is called for. A wilting plant in the morning is a warning of water need. Wilting between noon and 3:00 p.m. is not too significant as at that time increased light intensity as well as higher temperatures result in greater water loss from plants.

Usually a plant needs water when the soil surface appears "dry." Many soils look lighter in color when drying occurs. Dark colored soils do not show this color difference. Feeling the soil will serve to tell you if water is needed.

Never, never use cold water, but use water that is close to room temperature. The time of day is not of any importance, but a good many people prefer to water in the morning, probably more for their convenience than the plant's benefit.

Overwatering can result in rotting roots.

Applying water

Watering from below is much preferred because there is no chance of washing soil away from the plant stem. It also makes it easier to know when the soil is wet through. The simplest way to water from below is to stand the pots in a container with 2 or 3 inches of water and wait until the surface becomes damp before removing the pots.

A very practical and inexpensive self-watering device can be made using a glass wick to move water up into the soil. To make such a device take a 6 or 9 inch length of wick and pass it through the drainage hole, unravel it and cover the bottom of the pot with it (Figure 8). Then replace the soil leaving out the coarse drainage material at the bottom of the pot. Pack the soil down with your fingers to insure contact between wick and soil.

Next, with about 2 to 3 inches of wick extending from below, place the pot in a container of water, 2 to 3 inches

Figure 8. This is how the wick looks before the soil is put in. The other end of the wick is placed in a container of water. *Minnesota Extension Service.*

deep. If the water is too deep and the soil gets too wet, lower the water level. If the soil remains too dry, raise the water level. Be sure to keep water in the reservoir. If the soil becomes too dry, half submerge the pot in water for 30 minutes, then put it back into the reservoir refilled to its proper level.

This method keeps the soil moist continuously which is not always needed. By all means avoid this method with cacti and plants you are drying out to go into the rest period.

About once a month flush the pots that are using the wick method, by watering them thoroughly from the top to wash out any excess fertilizer salts which may have accumulated. The water that drains out of the drainage hole should be considered waste water.

Misting plants can be done with a little rubber bulb sprayer.

Vacation watering

All of us who go off from time to time wonder what to do with our plants while we are gone. The dogs and cats can be popped into the vet, but we know of very few plant sitters.

There are a number of systems that can be established and combined, depending on how long you will be gone.

For vacations of up to two weeks we have found a little device called the Floramatic Plant Watering Reservoir very helpful (Figure 9). It is a plastic reservoir that is filled with water and buried in the soil. A flow retarder at the top slows down water flow. We have found that with the retarder in position water lasted for an average of fifteen and a half days when used with a flowering geranium, *Pelargonium* spp. in a 5-inch plastic pot. Without the retarder, water flow was greater and the reservoir was emptied in an average of ten days.

Double potting can be useful during absences from home as well as at other times. This method (Figure 10) simply uses two pots, one inside the other, with damp sphagnum moss in between the two pots. The inner pot should be of porous material like clay, the outer one of non-porous material. The outer pot does not need a drainage hole. It is important to allow an inch or two between the sides and bottoms of the pots.

Figure 9. This Floramatic Plant Watering Reservoir waters the plant automatically. *Charles Balducci.*

Figure 10. A double potted plant. The inner pot is clay and the outer pot is filled with peat moss. *U.S.D.A.*

Another method good for about five to eight days is to water your plant well, then cover it with a plastic bag to reduce water loss. If the pot is clay or other porous material cover it to minimize water loss too (Figure 11).

For a long weekend you can keep a plant moist by using plastic tubing an inch in diameter. Plug the bottom end with cork or a bit of plastic held in place with a rubber band. Drill ⅛-inch holes up and down the tube every half inch, vertically in four rows. Put the tube into the pot, fill it with sand and then fill with water (Figure 12).

We have used all of these methods alone and in combination at one time or another with excellent results. It is a pleasure to return from a two-week trip to find all your plants in good condition.

Sheer curtains will help to lower the temperature and minimize evaporation but will not exclude the light that the plants need.

Figure 11. *(Left)* This plant is covered with a plastic bag to keep it from drying out while you are on vacation. *Virginia Polytechnic*

Figure 12. *(Below)* The end of this plastic tube is plugged up. Notice the row of holes along the tube. The tube is then filled with sand and then with water. It's another way of watering your plants while you're on vacation. *U.S.D.A.*

Chapter 4

POTS FOR PLANTS

Plants can be grown in just about any kind of container if provision is made for drainage. Even if no drainage takes place through drainage holes or porous walls, plants can be grown with an inch or two of pebbles or gravel at the bottom of the container. Watertight pots, however, are troublesome as any excess water will collect at the bottom of the pot and damage plant roots.

Pots

We prefer by far earthy red, unglazed clay pots as part of an honored tradition. These pots are long lasting, are almost impossible to waterlog and are pleasant to handle.

Plastic pots are available and we do use them frequently. They are lightweight, have drainage holes and require somewhat less watering than clay pots because the water does not evaporate through the sides of plastic. There are pre-seeded plastic pots available that come with their own plastic tray. All you have to do is to add water in order for the plants to germinate. Plastic pots in direct sunlight can heat up, and we have heard of plants being damaged.

Select the size pot that will comfortably accommodate the plant when it is full grown. Remember that a small seedling or a cutting will eventually be a large adult plant.

Small plants, for example, should live in small pots because there is less chance of the soil "souring" from overwatering.

Each pot should have a small saucer or pan beneath it to keep drainage water from running onto the floor or carpet. We find that some sand in the drainage container hastens evaporation of excess water.

We have mentioned double potting in the chapter on watering. It can also be used if you want to have a more attractive outer container on view. *But* too ornate an outer pot can detract from the main character of the play—the plant.

Planters

Planters are large containers used to hold a number of plants. They can be made of pottery, wood, brass or plastic. Many homes come with built-in planters in front of large windows, as room dividers or elsewhere. Planters that are built in are usually made of stone, concrete or metal and are both rustproof and waterproof.

Metal containers should be coated with asphalt emulsion to prevent toxicity, as well as to prevent rusting and to keep the container waterproof.

A petcock at the bottom of the planter is helpful in draining out excess water.

A 3-inch layer of drainage materials such as pebbles or gravel is required at the bottom of the planter. Above that, a ½-inch layer of charcoal prevents stagnation of any standing water. The remainder of the planter is filled with sphagnum moss or peat moss to within 3 to 4 inches of the top.

We prefer to pot doubled potted plants in clay containers in our planters. The clay permits water movement into the pots quite readily. We strongly recommend that plants with similar cultural requirements be planted in a planter, and that you check on available light when choosing your specimens.

Pots make it easier to remove diseased plants and plants that outgrow the planter. If you use pots of different sizes you can place the smaller ones on inverted pots to make them all level (Figure 13). Fill in the spaces between pots with more peat.

Small planters can be set up with plants not already potted if you like (Figure 14). Select plants that will grow at the same rate so that one will not shade another.

We have used a rather interesting modified planter (Figure

Figure 13. In this planter the smaller pots on the right are set on inverted pots to raise them to the same level as the larger pots. *U.S.D.A.*

15) made of plastic that is nicely suited for window still gardening.

The following plants seem to be especially well adapted to planters. There are others you may wish to try.

African violet, *Saintpaulia* spp.
Aucuba, *Aucuba japonica variegata*
chinese evergreen, *Aglaonema modestum*
croton, *Codiaeum variegatum*
dumb cane, *Dieffenbachia* spp
maranta, *Maranta* spp.
philodendrons, small, *Philodendron* spp.
pittosporum, *Pittosporum tobira*
pothos, *Scindapsus aureus*
screwpine, *Pandanus veitchei*
snake plant, *Sansevieria* spp.

Figure 14. These plants are being set directly in the planter and are not potted first. *U.S.D.A.*

Hanging baskets

We find hanging baskets best suited for areas of minimum traffic. It is disconcerting at the very best to bump your head on a clay pot, even if its resident is particularly attractive. We find our best spots to be on a patio, in the kitchen over the sink near the window, along the screens of porches or on a balcony.

These are a problem however. Watering is a job, and if your kitchen is not well ventilated, rising warm air adds to the difficulties.

We suggest for the indoors you use plastic pots to reduce moisture loss, and a plastic holder. For patio, porch or balcony you can use a mesh or woven basket lined with damp moss into which the plants go.

There are hanging baskets on the market with drainage holes. But watering hanging baskets is a bother, requiring a certain degree of physical agility combined with a real dedication to growing plants in hanging baskets. Our enthusiasm along these lines is tempered by the energy involved.

Figure 15. This plastic planter is excellent for putting your window space to good use. *Polestar Designs*

If you feel you do want to try your hand at basket gardening we have indicated in other parts of the book some of the plants adapted for this kind of indoor gardening. For convenience, here is a partial list of basket plants you might use.

begonia, *Begonia* spp.
Christmas cactus, *Zygocactus truncatus*
cissus, *Cissus* spp.
columnea, *Columnea* spp., vine types
English ivy, *Hedera helix*
ferns
fittonia, *Fittonia* spp.
flame violet, *Episcia* spp.
fuchsia, *Fuchsia* spp.
German ivy, *Senecio mikanioides*
ivy geraniums, *Pelargonium peltatum*
Kenilworth ivy, *Cymbalaria muralis*
lantana, *Lantana camara*
philodendron, vine types, *Philodendron* spp.

pothos, *Scindapsus aureus*
shamrock, *Oxalis* spp.
spider plant, *Chlorphytum capense*
strawberry geranium, *Saxifraga sarmentosa*
string of hearts, *Ceropegia woodii*
velvet plant, *Gynura aurantiaca*
wandering Jew, *Tradescantia fluminensis, Zebrina pendula*
wax plant, *Hoya carnosa*

Dish gardens

Dish gardens are creative and pure fun. Essentially, dish gardens are plantings of small, slow growing plants in open shallow dishes or containers. Often they are miniatures of a scene—a Japanese garden, a dwarfed forest scene, or even a pond, using a little piece of mirror for the pond.

These make-believe scenes are usually grown in dishes lacking drainage openings so watering is of major importance and overwatering a possibility. Always try to put ½-inch of charcoal, sand or gravel at the bottom to allow for drainage.

Carefully select plants with the same growth requirements for light and water.

After planting, spray the plants and soil until the soil is moist but not soaking. Then keep the dish in a shaded spot for about forty-eight hours, and move it into strong light for several days.

Watering is most efficient using a bulb sprayer and is required four to seven times a week.

Dish gardens with only a single species of plant are attractive in their own right and are particularly nice in offices where care is sporadic and weekends long (Figure 16).

Cacti are much favored for dish gardens as are succulents. Other well-suited plants include:

African violet, *Saintpaulia* spp.
aloe, *Aloe* spp.
boxwood, dwarf, *Buxus sempervirens*
bromeliads
Chinese evergreen, *Aglaonema modestum*
coleus, *Coleus* spp.
deer's tongue, *Gasteria* spp.

dracaena, *Dracaena* spp.
dumb cane, *Dieffenbachia* spp.
English ivy, small varieties, *Hedera helix*
evergreen seedlings
ferns, small, dwarf, and seedlings
fig, *Ficus pumila*
fittonia, *Fittonia* spp.
geranium, dwarf, *Pelargonium* spp.
Irish moss, *Helxine soleiroli*
kalanchoe, *Kalanchoe* spp.
maranta, *Maranta* spp.
mosses
palm, miniature and dwarf
peperomia, *Peperomia* spp.
philodendron, young, *Philodendron* spp.
pilea, *Pilea* spp.
podocarpus, *Podocarpus macrophylla*
pothos, *Scindapsus aureus*
screwpine, *Pandanus veitchei*
snake plant, *Sansevieria* spp.
spindletree, *Euonymus* spp.
strawberry geranium, *Saxifraga sarmentosa*
wandering Jew, *Tradescantia fluminensis,* and *Zebrina
    pendula*
wax plant, *Hoya carnosa*

Figure 16.   This dish garden contains a single philodendron plant. *Arnold Krochmal*

Chapter 5

PROPAGATION OF PLANTS

There is a lot of fun and pleasure, and a feeling of satisfaction, in propagating a favorite plant to give someone as a living gift, or to increase the number of plant people in your home. We sometimes find our plant family has increased so much that they—and us— get a bit crowded!

Seed or Cuttings?

A number of simple techniques can be used with ease to propagate plants in the home. The only tools needed are a sharp pocket knife and a pair of small pruning shears.

Methods of propagation are divided into two basic categories: sexual (using seeds), and vegetative (using parts of one plant to grow other plants).

The method selected, seed or cuttings, will usually be related to the plant, because some can be propagated by one means and not the other, and some by both. If seed and vegetative means are both useable for a particular plant, then consider the other points involved.

Growing plants from seeds can result in some variability in the new plants because each seed will have half of the male parent's characteristics and half of the female parent's characteristics.

Some plants produce large quantities of seeds, others very few. Some plants require hand pollination from the male flower to the female flower at the right time. We should note that the home plant grower may find crossing of plants a very fulfilling hobby.

Plantings grown from cuttings completely resemble the plant from which they were taken. They are totally a child of the source plant.

Propagating Structures

An important problem in propagating plants by seed or cuttings is maintaining a high moisture level in the air. Some kind of simple structure is needed that keeps moisture in but allows air circulation.

For cuttings we often use 8-inch plastic pots. We close the drainage hole at the bottom of the pot with clay or putty and fill the pot with vermiculite or perlite. Then we take a 2- or 3-inch pot and close the drainage hole as before. The small pot is then placed in the center of the large pot and filled with water. Cuttings are planted in the moistened medium in the larger pot (Figure 17).

Blocks of plastic foam can also be used to root cuttings in (Figure 18). Dampen the block and wrap the top and sides in aluminum foil. Then use a scissors to cut slits in the foam and insert the cuttings in these. As the foam dries out, add more water to keep it moist.

A round or square aquarium makes a very neat propagating unit for both seeds and cuttings. The bottom should be covered with about an inch of gravel for drainage, topped with 3 to 4 inches of vermiculite or perlite. When the media is moistened, seeds can be sown or cuttings placed in position. A piece of glass or polyethylene placed over the top completes the propagating structure. If light is desired, a small aquarium lamp can be used, with an incandescent tube of 25 watts or less, with a glass top *only* (Figure 19).

Simple propagating mini-greenhouses can be made using large freezer bags of polyethylene. An inch of pebbles is first put into the bag and then three inches or so of vermiculite or potting mix. After water is added and either seeds planted or cuttings placed (Figure 20), the bags are fastened carefully (Figure 21) without disturbing the cuttings. The completed mini-greenhouse can be placed on a window with a northern

Figure 17.   The smaller inner pot contains water and keeps the cuttings in the large pot moist. *Virginia Polytechnic Institute.*

exposure. No further watering is needed until the seeds are germinated or the cuttings examined after eight weeks.

Cuttings will usually root in from eight to ten weeks. After eight weeks gently open the bag and remove a cutting. If a number of roots ½- to 1-inch long have formed (Figure 22) the cutting is ready to be potted. Before potting however, condition the plants to room humidity by keeping the bag open for increasing periods of time during a week. Keep the soil mixture moist during this period. Any cuttings which have not rooted, but are still alive, should be kept in the closed plastic bag, and examined every two weeks for roots. Any cuttings which have lost their leaves or decayed at the base should be tossed out.

Rooting Media

There is virtually no limit to the combination of materials that can be used for rooting cuttings and germinating seeds.

Figure 18. Plastic foam blocks can be used for rooting cuttings. The block on the right has been thoroughly wet, then wrapped in foil (middle) and the cuttings inserted. *Univ. of Minnesota Agr. Ext. Ser.*

The major materials, all of which are readily found in garden stores as well as many supermarkets and five-and-tens, are sand, soil, sphagnum moss, peat moss, bermiculite and perlite. The last two are sterile when bought.

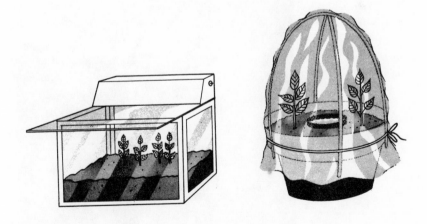

Figure 19. *(Right)* Bent metal hangers are placed over the top of the container and a plastic bag or sheet is slipped over the frame and tied in place. *(Left)* This aquarium with a glass top makes an excellent propagating unit. The 25-watt fluorescent tube provides extra light. *University of California Extension Service.*

Figure 20. A plastic bag is prepared with an inch layer of pebbles and several inches of vermiculite and is dampened. Then the cuttings or seeds are set in place. *U.S.D.A.*

Figure 21. *(Left)* The mini-greenhouse bag is closed and placed in a cool window with partial sunlight. *U.S.D.A.*

Figure 22. If a cutting has well-formed roots from ½–1 inch long it is ready for transplanting. *U.S.D.A.*

Fibrous peat moss and soil you may have gotten yourself should be passed through a coarse screen (Figure 23) to remove larger particles, twigs and stones. The next step is to mix the peat with sand and soil in a ratio you find best. We use equal parts of each of these components.

The moist mixture can be sterilized at 180°F. in a metal pan in the oven for one-half hour. When the mix is cooled, add

Figure 23. Sift the soil and sand through a screen before preparing your potting mix. *U.S.D.A.*

vermiculite or perlite in any amount you feel best. We use the same amount as each of the three other parts.

When the mix is ready, add water and combine well (Figure 24). The soil is ready for use when you squeeze a handful and only a few drops of water squeeze out. Be careful in handling the hot sand, soil or mixes and containers as they can cause severe burns. Use a hot pad for safety.

Clay pots, and ceramic jugs and aquariums made of a single piece of glass, can be sterilized in the same way. We are a little leery of plastic containers in the oven and prefer another method for them. We rinse plastic with boiling water, followed by a thorough scrubbing with soap and water and a series of cold water rinses.

Hormones

Plant hormones are available at garden stores and flower shops to help stimulate root formation. The end of a cutting or

Figure 24. Water the potting mix until it is moist but not soggy. *U.S.D.A.*

stem of a leaf is dipped in water, then into the hormone powder, and the excess knocked off by gently tapping the cutting.

Cuttings

A cutting is a piece of an older plant such as a stem, leaf or root used to produce a new plant exactly like the parent plant. The procedure usually begins with the separation of the selected plant part from the parent. The exception is air-layering, which we will discuss a little later.

Most house plants usually can be readily propagated by cuttings. Success in rooting cuttings depends on the survival of the cuttings until they grow roots and leaves, and keeping them from dying until these growths appear.

Material selected for cuttings should be healthy and free from insect and disease damage. It should be taken from plants that have no flowers because plants in flower do not root easily.

A quick and simple way of testing material if you have

enough is to snap a piece of stem between your fingers (Figure 25). A crisp popping sound indicates the material is ready for rooting.

Kinds of cuttings

Leaf, stem and canes are the sources of materials for cuttings.

Stem cuttings or slips (Figure 26) are made from strong lateral or terminal shoots. Plants propagated by this method include everblooming begonia, cactus, coleus, German ivy, philodendron and wax plants. A good stem cutting is 3 to 6 inches long. Using a sharp knife, cut at a slight angle just below the node, or joints, in the stem. Remove the leaves from the bottom 2 or 3 inches and insert in the rooting medium.

Leaf bud cuttings are made by cutting a segment of stem with a leaf and the bud in the axil of the leaf. The cutting is planted horizontally below the surface of the propagating media (Figure 27). Philodendron, pothos, wax plant are among those propagated this way.

Figure 25.   Only plant material that snaps crisply is healthy enough for cuttings. *U.S.D.A.*

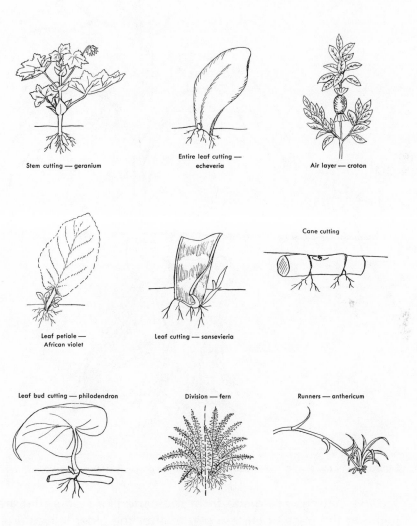

Stem cutting — geranium

Entire leaf cutting —
echeveria

Air layer — croton

Leaf petiole —
African violet

Leaf cutting — sansevieria

Cane cutting

Leaf bud cutting — philodendron

Division — fern

Runners — anthericum

Figure 26.   Types of propagation illustrated. *U.S.D.A.*

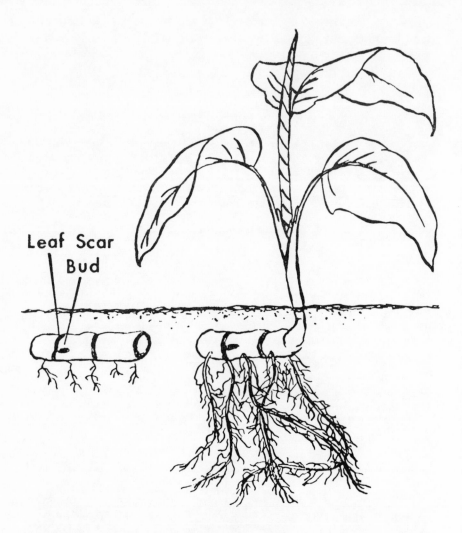

Figure 27. This shows a leaf bud cutting planted properly. *Pennsylvania Ext. Ser.*

Cane cuttings are made from the cane-like stems that are found at the base of certain plants after the older leaves drop off. These canes are cut into pieces with two leaf scars per piece. The cutting (Figure 26) is planted horizontally just below the soil surface, with the dormant eye facing upward. Chinese evergreen, dracaena, and dumb cane can be handled in this way.

An entire leaf is used for stonecrop, hen-and-chickens, and snake plant (Figure 26). Snake plant and the palmleaf begonia can be cut into two to four sections and used to produce several plants.

Division

A number of plants form clumps, such as ferns, snake plant, some African violets, prayer plant, English ivy and everblooming begonia. These clumps can be separated into several smaller plants (Figure 26).

The African violet in Figure 28 has multiple crowns or growing points and has been divided into five separate plants as shown in Figure 29. Be sure to leave as much soil as possible on the roots during the operation.

Air-Layering

Air-layering is spectacular but not too difficult technique to master. It is used with woody stemmed plants such as the rubber plant, croton, fiddleleaf fig and schefflera.

A one-year-old stem is cut halfway through (Figure 30) and the cut held open with a small wedge, or the bark is scraped

Figure 28. This African violet has multiple crowns or growing points and can be divided into several plants. See Figure 29 for separate plants. *Univ. of Minnesota Ext. Ser.*

Figure 29. Five separate African violet plants are obtained by dividing an African violet with multiple crowns or growing points. *Univ. of Minnesota Ext. Ser.*

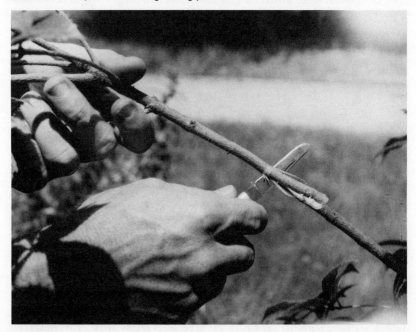

Figure 30. This stem is being prepared for air-layering. *U.S.D.A.*

½-inch wide around the stem. Moist sphagnum moss is tied in a ball around the cut (Figure 31) and covered with plastic (Figure 32). Friction tape is used to bind the plastic to make an airtight package the size of an orange or large apple (Figure 33). New roots will form in the plastic ball; when you can see them, cut the plant off below the new root area and pot.

This method can be used to reshape tall leggy plants which have lost their bottom leaves. The air-layering is done right below the remaining leaves (Figure 26), and the ungainly stem is cut back to 8 or 10 inches. New shoots will grow to make a more attractive plant and you will then have two plants.

Runners

Runners are shoots or stems which grow along the surface of the ground and which often produce clusters of leaves at their nodes, or joints.

Among the house plants which produce runners are strawberry geranium, spider plant, Boston fern, mother-of-thousands, apostle plant and pick-a-back plant.

Figure 31. Moist sphagnum moss is wrapped around the cut and is tied loosely in place. *U.S.D.A.*

Figure 32. A piece of plastic is then wrapped around the moist sphagnum moss. *U.S.D.A.*

Figure 33. Bind the plastic in place with some friction tape. *U.S.D.A.*

In the wild, runners produce new plants when they lie on the damp soil. In the home a little help is called for, by one of two methods.

When a plant produces runners, fill several flower pots with your favorite prepared soil mix. Place each leafy cluster on the soil in one of the pots. Then use an open, non-spring clothes pin, crossed wooden matches or toothpicks to hold the runner in place. Keep the soil moist and the pot in subdued light. In about a month roots should develop sufficiently to permit cutting the "umbilical" cord of the runner from the mother plant to the young plant (Figure 26).

The second method is to cut off the leafy cluster with a portion of the runner and root it.

Tap Water

As kids in New York we found early in life that the top of a carrot or a piece of sweet potato could be grown at no cost into, what was for us, a miraculous plant all of our own.

An empty pint or quart jar was the container most frequently used because some neighbor in the apartment house would let us have one free. In the 1930s and early 1940s the Great Depression made cash for non-essentials pretty scarce. Using tap water we made a series of bottle gardens that gave us hours of enjoyment for free.

Almost any kind of container can be used (Figure 34) as long as it is waterproof. Bottles and jars of any shape and size will do well. A large number of plants can be propagated in this way (Table 1).

Table 1. A list of plants which can be propagated readily in water.

African violet	grape ivy
aglaonema	hibiscus
aluminum plant	impatiens
aucuba	ivy
avocado	peperomia
carrot	philodendron
coleus	sweet potato
geranium	wax begonia

Figure 34. Several cuttings can be propagated in each bottle of water. *U.S.D.A.*

The first step is to wash the container with hot soapy tap water, then rinse several times and fill the bottle to an inch or two of the top. Then cut small branch or stem from the mother plant with a sharp knife just below the point at which a leaf grows. Next cut off the top of the cutting, leaving a stem about 8 to 12 inches long, and put in the water. If leaves extend under water, remove them.

Keep the water level at its original height and once a month wash the bottles well to reduce algae growth. Rotate the container in the light to encourage uniform growth.

Seeds

A large number of house plants can be propagated by sexual means from seed. The list includes African violet, begonia, cacti, coleus, cyclamen, fuchsia, gloxinia and a great many more.

Seed can be bought for many of these and in some cases can be obtained at home. Garden club members often trade seeds with each other, a worthwhile program activity.

Growing plants from seed is a longer process than growing them by vegetative methods. However, it is an easy way to grow a larger number than is possible from a limited source of cuttings and runners. Using seed makes it practical for a plant enthusiast to start several pots of seed in late summer or early fall in order to give young plants to friends and guests during the December holiday season.

Soil mixture

Much the same materials used for cuttings are used for seeds (Figure 35). Variations are an individual matter based on personal preference. Sterilization follows the same procedure.

Containers

Flats of wood, flower pots or trays of heatproof material 3 to 4 inches deep can be used to germinate seed. If pots are used the drainage hole should be covered to keep the soil from running out. We use a piece of paper towel folded over several times. A piece of broken pot or some large pieces of gravel will do equally well if you have them handy.

Figure 35. Sand, soil and peat moss are combined to form a potting mix. *U.S.D.A.*

If you are using seed flats cover the bottom with 4 or 5 sheets of newspaper to keep the soil mix from running out. Plastic flats or trays do not require this step. The containers are treated as for cuttings to keep them as free of disease as is possible.

Small plaques of pressed peat moss can be used very satisfactorily. We just put one of the plaques (Figure 36) into a

Figure 36. This pressed peat moss plaque is placed in a pot and moistened, then a seed is added. *U.S.D.A.*

styrofoam cup and then add sufficient water to swell the plaque. After about half an hour the excess water is drained off and the seeds planted. A small sandwich bag completes this mini-propagating ocntrivance.

Planting

The container is filled to within ½-inch of the top with the soil mix, and then pressed down firmly with the knuckles and the thumbs along the edges (Figure 37). Sprinkle about ¼-inch of fine vermiculite over the surface. Moisten the soil by placing the container in a shallow pan of water until the vermiculite is moist or use a fine sprinkler from the top (Figure 38). If any deep depressions appear, fill them up and pack down again.

Once the vermiculite is moist, make slight depressions ⅛-inch to ¼-inch deep in one or more rows in the surface of the soil. Each depression or row, if you make several, should be about 2 inches from its neighbor.

Figure 37. Press the potting mix with the hands to make sure the pot is filled because it will pack down when moistened. *U.S.D.A.*

Sow the seeds by gently tapping the seed packet (Figure 39) with the forefinger so that the seeds are somewhat scattered in the row. If the seeds are sown too close together the seedlings will be spindly and weak.

Small seeds such as African violet and begonia are left uncovered as they are likely not to germinate if they are covered. Larger seeds are covered with vermiculite or screened sphagnum moss until they are just hidden and gently pressed down so the seeds are in contact with the soil. Last, cover the container with a polyethylene plastic freezer bag (Figure 40) to minimize moisture loss. No further water should be needed until the bag is removed.

Seedling care

The container may be placed in a window sill out of the direct rays of the sun. The best temperature range is 65–75°F.

Some plants, like coleus and geraniums, are sun lovers and from a week after the plastic is removed they should be kept in direct sun. Others, such as African violet and begonia, thrive in bright light but not direct sun.

Figure 38.   Use a sprinkler to moisten the potting mix. *U.S.D.A.*

As soon as the first leaves are formed the plastic bag can be removed and the seedlings transplanted (Figure 41), either one to a 3-inch pot, or several to a flat, using your own favorite soil mixture.

Be sure the plants are well watered but not to the point where the water runs out of the bottom of the container.

Special methods for some cacti and succulents

Although most cacti and succulents can be propagated readily by seed, there are some vegetative methods worth considering.

When we lived in Arizona and New Mexico we were able to collect numbers of these plants which originated vegetatively.

Offsets

Offsets are plants produced by other plants. Sometimes these new plants are produced on the body of the older plant, as with *Echinocereus* and *Echinopsis.* In other plants, including *Agave, Aloe, Sedum* and *Haworthia,* a circle of young plants is pro-

Figure 39. When sowing seeds hold the pack in one hand and gently tap the pack with a finger of the other hand. *U.S.D.A.*

duced around the base of the mother plant attached by their roots. Some offsets are produced on leaves as is found on *Bryophyllum.* Any such offsets can be separated from the parent plant and potted.

Cuttings

Leaves of *Aloe, Sedum,* and others can be used to propagate new plants. Carefully cut off a healthy leaf, lay it on a pot of sand and peg it down along the edges using toothpicks. The leaf will gradually dry up and a new plant appear at the point where the leaf had been attached to the old plant. Branching succulents and cacti can be propagated by cuttings made of parts of the branches and trunks.

Some of the *Euphorbias, Opuntias,* and *Echevarias* can be propagated by simply cutting a piece of a branch and putting it into a suitable rooting medium. Other cacti, including the *Echevaria* and the *Cereus,* can be propagated by cutting off the top of the stem and placing it in sand. Such cut tops produce series of plantlets which in turn can be potted.

All cuttings should be kept in a cool, well ventilated place for three or four days after cutting and before potting to encourage callus formation, the soft tissue which forms over the cut surface of a stem from which the new roots develop.

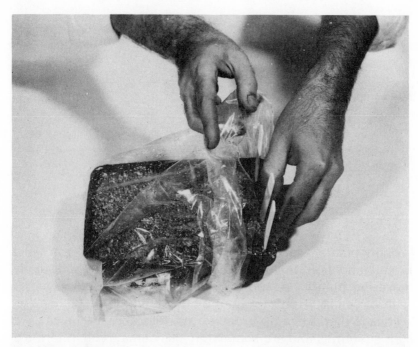

Figure 40.   Cover the flat or pot with a plastic bag to keep the soil moist. *U.S.D.A.*

Figure 41.   When the seedlings form true leaves they are ready to transplant to 3-inch pots. *U.S.D.A.*

Chapter 6

FOLIAGE PLANTS

Foliage plants are those grown mainly for their attractive leaves although many of them will bear flowers. Usually, flowering plants are more eye-catching, but in a way their span of beauty is shorter than a foliage plant.

Foliage plants are, in broad terms, less demanding of strict light quantities and are somewhat less demanding in terms of fertilizer needs. They are excellent for use in public areas where the conditions for growth may be less than ideal for flowering plants.

There is a broad enough spectrum of growth needs for this class of plants to provide a variety for just about any growing conditions you may have in your home.

aphelandra, *Aphelandra* spp. (Figure 42).
Small evergreen shrubs with dark green leaves. One species has vivid white veins and showy red or yellow flowers borne on spikes, usually flowering in fall. After flowering the plant is cut back to 1-2 pairs of stems. It prefers indirect sunlight but will do well in moderate to dim light.

It should be kept moist and prefers a minimum temperature of 65°F. with a low humidity. It is propagated by cuttings and seed. A rich and organic soil is recommended.

aralia, *Polyscias* spp. (*Aralia* spp.).
These are descendents of aromatic shrubs from tropical Asia. The plants are very slow growers and can be kept to a suitable house size.

Figure 42. Left to right: *Dracaena sanderiana, Dracaena fragrans, Aphelandra squarrosa. U.S.D.A.*

The foliage varies greatly, some varieties having finely cut leaves. The plants require bright light, a minimum temperature of 65°F. and a continually moist soil. Propagation is by cuttings.

P. balfouriana marginata has green leaves with white borders.

P. guilfoylei victoriae. This graceful lacy plant has grayish-green leaflets with white borders. Known as wild coffee in tropical America.

baby's tears, Irish moss, *Helxine soleirolii.*

This plant brings home the problem of common names. The last time we wrote about Irish moss was in our book about natural dyes and the Irish moss in that book was a seaweed, totally unrelated to this one.

This is a small creeping plant with delicate small leaves. It grows rapidly and will cover the soil surface of a container with a growth resembling moss. Thus the name.

Although the plant prefers bright light it will grow in partial shade. It prefers a cool temperature around 50°F. and ample soil moisture. It will occasionally die down to the soil surface, rest, and then begin growth again.

beefstock plant, blood-leaf, *Iresine* supp. (Figure 43).

There are two species, one with red stems and leaves of red and gold, the other with green leaves and gold veins. Both flourish in full sun, with a temperature of about 60°F. and moist soil.

During the winter, supplementary light will help keep the plant vigorous. Both are propagated by cuttings made in late summer and early fall.

caladium, *Caladium* supp.

Caladiums are increasing in popularity because of the beauty of their foilage and the modest amount of care they require. The evergreen, arrow-shaped leaves have patterns of pink, white, green, red and yellow.

Figure 43. Left to right: *Coleus blumei, Dracaena sanderiana, Iresine herbstii.* U.S.D.A.

Propagated by tubers, the plants should be started in February or March in a rich organic soil 2 or 3 to a 6-inch pot, each tuber 2 inches deep.

Water lightly, then store the pots in a warm spot, about 60°F. After 2 to 3 weeks, when roots have begun to grow, move the pots to indirect light or a semi-shaded spot for the summer, increasing watering at the same time. Usual summer temperatures and humidity are fine.

About October or November begin lengthening the period between waterings. The leaves will dry up and the tubers will go into dormancy. The plants should then be stored in a cool area, such as a basement, with a temperature around 60°F. In the spring repot the tubers and begin the cycle again.

calathea, *Calathea* spp. (Figure 44).

These are often confused with some of the marantas which they strongly resemble and some garden writers ignore the confusion that exists.

C. illustris is thought to be closely related to *C. roseopicta,*

Figure 44. Left to right: *Calathea ornata, Podocarpus macrophylla, Aglaonema commutatus.* U.S.D.A.

but *C. illustris* has leaves that are white and the underside red. Flowers are purple.

C. ornata can have green-purplish blades 2 feet long.

C. roseo-picta grows to 6 inches or so in height, with long leaves that are dark green above with a red mid-rib and splotches of red. The bottom is purple and the yellow flower spike is 3 inches long. Sometimes grown as *Maranta bicolor.*

C. zebrina, zebra plant has leaves 6–12 inches wide and 1–2 feet long, with a striped alternating pattern that gives it the name zebra plant.

cast iron plant, aspidistra, *Aspidistra lurida.*

The ability to survive under rugged conditions gives this plant its common name. There is a white-striped variety and a variety with large dark green glossy leaves.

It is not too fussy about soils and will grow in almost any well drained soil. It will grow as well in the bright light of an eastern exposure and the shade of dark corners. It likes a generous water supply and a temperature of 60–70°F.

It is propagated by seed, or by division in the spring.

Chinese evergreen, *Aglaonema modestum (A. simplex).*

This easy-care plant grows from 2-3 feet tall and thrives under pretty·poor conditions, even with poor light. Its shiny dark green leaves grow at the end of cane-like stems. The plants prefer a soil rich in organic matter and prefer good light if possible and little water. The plants will also grow in water. If the plant becomes too spindly and bare looking, cut the top off and root it in water for a new plant. It is propagated by cuttings. Several species are sold. *A. commutatus* has a greenish-white spathe and produces red and purple berries (Figure 44). *A. pseudo-bracteatum* is by far the most exciting of the group. It has long leaves that are variegated light and dark green, yellow and creamy white and white stems. *A. simplex* is the most common form and has dark green narrow leaves with depressed veins.

chocolate plant, *Pseudcranathemum alatum* (Figure 45).

This low-growing plant is tropical in origin. The large thick leaves are oval and heavily veined. The leaves may grow low

Figure 45. *Pseuderanthemum alatum*. Arnold Krochmal

and droop over the edges of the pot. It should be allowed to dry out slightly between waterings, should have indirect sunlight and a temperature of 60-65°F.

cissus, *Cissus* spp.

These climbers are related to the grape family and all have tendrils. The group prefers bright light but not direct sunlight. They like plenty of water and a fine spray once a week or more will help. A minimum temperature of 60°F. is required.

The more vigorous varieties should have something on which to climb. Hanging baskets provide an ideal home for all types. Propagation is by cuttings.

C. rhombifolia, grape ivy, is more compact than the others.

C. discolor, begonia ivy, has red shoots and brightly colored leaves, purple below and multicolored above. This is by far the most vivid of the cissus group.

C. antartica, kangaroo vine, and the miniature kangaroo vine will tolerate lower temperatures than the others.

coleus, *Coleus* spp. (Figure 43).

One of the group of durable, easy-to-grow house plants admired for its vivid and brilliantly colored foliage. Leaves vary from red and green to yellow, pink, brown, purple, orange and combinations, and have scalloped edges.

The colors *do* require full sun to develop. A warm temperature of 60°F. and higher are preferred and a moist soil. However, the plants will survive chilling and overwatering. Pinch the tips of the plants frequently to induce compact, bushy growth.

Propagation is easy. A cutting with a couple of leaves in a glass of water is all that is required. Seeds may be sown as well.

columnea, *Columnea* spp. (Figures 46, 47).

These have upright forms as well as low spreading or trailing ones. They have bright tube-shaped flowers that can be orange, red or yellow. The velvety leaves are covered with purple hairs. The vine types are suitable for hanging baskets. *C. hirta* and *C. evlo* are favorites. *C. hirta* is called the goldfish plant because the bright orange flowers are thought to resemble goldfish.

These should be kept moist and requires a high humidity. They prefer direct or indirect sunlight. The soil should be high in added peat moss, manure or leaf mold. They should have a cool night temperature of 55–60°F.

Figure 46. *Columnea evlo.* Arnold, Krochmal

Figure 47. *Columnea hirta.* Arnold Krochmal

croton, *Codiaeum variegatum* (Figure 48).

Very durable tropical shrubs with a great range of adaptability. We grew these as shrubs at our home in the Virgin Islands and later on in Raleigh, North Carolina. They thrived in both places.

The leaves vary greatly in shape as well as color and are evergreen. The colors can include patterns of yellow, scarlet, pink, white and green.

After they reach 3 feet in height, we keep them outside. Although they like full sun 3 seasons of the year, they cannot tolerate direct sunlight in the summer. They like a moist soil and an occasional spraying of their foliage.

As the plants grow older the lower leaves may fall, leaving the lower trunk nude and ungainly looking. Just as we suggested for the rubber plant, the croton top can be air-layered to form new roots, then cut from the old plant and repotted to form a new plant.

dracaena, *Dracaena* spp.

Dracaenas grow slowly, and are usually bought from garden shops and florists. The plants retain their foliage for long

Figure 48.   Left to right: *Sansevieria trifaciata, Codiaeum variegatum, Ficus elastica.*
U.S.D.A.

periods. They thrive in bright light in the fall and winter, but
partial shade and high humidity during the summer. A minimum
temperature of 60–65°F, is best.

D. dermensis warnecki, Warnecki dracaena, has gray-green
leaves with white stripes down the center (Figure 49).

D. fragrans massangeana, massange dracaena, is distinguished by longitudinal yellow and greenish white stripes on a
green leaf.

D. godseffiana, spotted dracaena, is the most common and
has dark green leaves with white spots.

D. godseffiana "Florida Beauty" is a variegated form with
white markings.

D. hookeriana, Roth dracaena, is a very durable plant with
dark green leaves and a waxy leaf margin (Figure 49).

D. sandereana, Sanders dracaena, has broad white bands on
its foliage (Figure 49).

D. sandereana "Margaret Berkery" has waxey deep green
leaves with a white stripe in the center of each leaf (Figure
49).

Figure 49. Dracaenas can vary in appearance from one variety and species to another. **1**. *Dracaena sanderiana* "Margaret Berkery" **2**. *Dracaena sanderiana* **3**. *Dracaena hookeriana* "rothiana" **4**. *Dracaena godseffiana* "Florida Beauty" **5**. *Dracaena dermensis warnecki* (Univ. of Minn. Ext. Ser.)

There is a tendency for leaves to drop off with age, leaving a plucked chicken effect. If this happens, start a new plant by air-layering the top of the plant. Propagation is by cuttings.

dumb cane, tuftroot, *Dieffenbachia* spp.

Dumb cane is one of the most spectacular of house plants. It is grown for its striking and luxuriant foliage. Most species as they become older tend to lose their lower leaves and the plant becomes less attractive. If this happens, simply cut off the top of the plant leaving 6 inches of stem. New growth will develop.

The origin of the name is charming, if somewhat scary. When we lived in the Virgin Islands a story was told if you chewed the plant you would lose your voice. On Martinique, local residents claim that the earlier Indian inhabitants made a paralizing poison from the plant that was used on arrows.

The plants will tolerate dim light but much prefer bright light, a minimum temperature of 60°F., low humidity and moderate drying of the soil between waterings. Overwatering will often result in root rotting.

D. amoena can tolerate lower temperatures than the others. It has white splotches along the veins (Figure 50).

D. bausei has white and dark green blotches on very light green leaves.

D. picta (Figure 51), spotted dum cane, is an outstanding

Figure 50. Left to right: *Dieffenbachia picta* "Rudolph Roehrs," *Dieffenbachia amoena, Ficus pandurata.* U.S.D.A.

cultivar (a plant that has been produced only under cultivation) with dark green leaves displaying creamy blotches.

D. picta "Rudolph Roehrs," Roehrs dumb cane, has leaves of pale green blotched with white and borders of dark green (Figure 50).

dwarf boxwood, *Buxus sempervirens.*

It is odd to think of the boxwood familiar to us as a common hedge plant growing as a potted plant.

A dwarf variety can be potted, and with its shiny green leaves and compact sturdy growth, it adds a real touch of the outdoors to the home. These plants require heavy pruning to keep them small. A moist, well drained soil, night temperatures of 50–60°F, are best.

Propagation is by cuttings in the spring. When plants outgrow their convenient dwarf size they can go outdoors if you have a yard, or to a friend who does.

Figure **51**. *Dieffenbachia* *picta.*
U.S.D.A.

English ivy, *Hedera helix.*

English ivy, which is available in a great range of varieties, makes an excellent house plant. Some of the newer, small leaf kinds make bushier, more compact plants than the large leaf types.

Variegated varieties are available but we have found them more troublesome to grow than the green leaf types.

Ivies prefer a cool location to discourage attacks by insects, low humidity, and bright light to direct sunlight, although they will tolerate poor light.

When the plants are small we suggest you pinch off the ends of the shoots to encourage a bushier growth. An attractive effect can be achieved by training the vines against a small trellis or a plant stake in the pot.

Propagation is by stem cuttings at any time of the year.

H. helix conglomerata, an upright form has small crowded leaves.

false aralia, *Dizygotheca elegantissima.*

A resemblance to some aralias can lead to confusion here. The false aralia is a graceful looking plant, with compound red-brown leaves. They are usually single stemmed and grow to about 18 inches in height. The plants do best with indirect light, moist soil and a minimum temperature of 65°F.

The plants tend to suffer if the soil remains dry. Propagation is by cuttings, preferably taken in the spring.

fat headed lizzie, tree ivy, *Fatshedera lizei.*

An unusual plant, said to be a cross between English ivy *Hedera* and *Fatsia.*

The plants are climbers and should be supported on a trellis or stick. The star-shaped leaves are 5-lobed, dark shining green. There is also a variegated variety.

They prefer partial shade or indirect sunlight and cool locations, and good moisture except in the winter and watering should be somewhat reduced.

The plants can be propagated by air-layering and cuttings.

Fatshedera japonica has leathery dark green leaves with 5 lobes, and is evergreen (Figure 61).

fittonia, silvervein fittonia, *Fittonia verschaffelti argyroneura* (Figure 52).

This should have a medium or high humidity, a warm temperature and bright light, but not direct sunlight. The soil should be kept moist as the plant will wilt if the soil dries out. This plant spreads out and has oval leaves with silvery veins, thus the name. The soil needs to have peat moss or manure added. It should be fertilized every six to eight weeks.

Figure 52. *Fittonia   verschaffeltii argyroneura.* Arnold Krochmal

flame violet, *Episcia* spp. (Figure 53).

This low growing dwarf plant resembles the African violet and is related to it. It has hanging or spreading branches, velvety oval leaves and spreads by runners. Its small pink to red flowers are fringed on the edges. Fine for hanging baskets. It likes high temperatures 65–75°F. and high humidity. Care is similar to African violets but it needs a little more light than African violets. As the plant gets older it may develop stiff woody branches. It is propagated by leaf cuttings, plantlets, runners and seeds.

flamingo flower, *Anthurium* spp.

Some species are grown for their flowers, others for their foliage. *A. andraenum* (Figure 54), has shiny flowers that are white, pink or red. *A. crystallinum* (Figure 54), has velvety green leaves with silver veins. *A. scherzerianum* has waxy shield-shaped leaves with a flaming pink pulpit shaped flower. It will not outgrow a 3-inch pot for years.

All species should be kept moist; watering from the bottom is

Figure 53. Left to right: African violet, *Saintpaulia* spp., Cape primrose, *Strepto-carpus* spp., flame violet, *Episcia* spp. U.S.D.A.

Figure 54. flamingo flower, left, *Anthurium andraenum,* right, *Anthurium crystalinum.* U.S.D.A.

recommended. It should be grown in a coarse and porous soil, high in humus, in indirect or subdued sunlight. It needs a warm night temperature of 60°F., thrives in high humidity and should be sprayed once a week until the flower buds form. The aerial roots which appear below the base of each leaf should be wrapped in sphagnum moss and kept moist.

The most practical way of increasing the plants is by division, repotting in a mix rich of peat or organic matter.

German ivy, water ivy, parlor ivy, *Senecio mikanioides.*

This is a climber with small yellow flowers, and can withstand night temperatures as low as 50°F. It thrives in bright sun during the winter; in summer it does better with a little less sun.

In Jamaica we have seen a really beautiful *Senecio* with vivid orange flowers and in Mexico we saw *Senecio confusus* with handsome red blooms. Both of these deserve distribution as handsome house plants.

All can be propagated by seed as well as cuttings.

gold dust plant, aucuba, *Aucuba japonica variegata.*

This shrub grows to 3 feet in height and has glossy gold spotted leaves and clusters of red berries. It prefers a well drained soil that is kept moist and a temperature of 60–70°F., but below 75°F. It prefers the partial shade of an east, west or south window though it will tolerate some sun and bright light. It will survive variable temperature and poor light.

It is propagated by 6-inch cuttings which root easily and readily in a jar of water, with about 1/3 of a cutting in the water, the rest above it. When the roots are about an inch or two long, pot the new plant in a rich mixture of ½ soil and ½ peat.

When we lived in Raleigh we had an aucuba that began as a 2-foot tall plant, and in our backyard in two years in semi-shade grew to 5 feet in height.

ivy arum, pothos, *Scindapsus aureus (Pothos aureus)* (Figure 55).

This is a climbing plant that can be confused with the heart-

Figure 55.   Left to right: *Phoenix* spp., *Nephrolepsis* spp., *Scindapsus aureus.* U.S.D.A.

leaf philodendron. It can be distinguished by its ridged stem which the philodendron does not have.

This ivy requires a constantly moist soil, a minimum temperature of 65°F. and can be grown in light varying from bright, for green varieties, to very low. The variegated variety, silver marble, requires a temperature above 70°F.

Devil's ivy is a variety with glossy green leaves and some yellow spotting. Tricolor has green leaves with yellow and red variegation, and the marble varieties are variegated with white. These plants can be propagated from stem cuttings.

Japanese aralia, *Fatsia japonica (Aralia japonica* or *A. sieboldii).*

A bushy evergreen with deep glossy green-lobed leaves borne on long stalks. We think this plant deserves a lot more attention as an indoor plant than it gets because it is hardy and can carry on despite adverse growing conditions.

It will do well in semi-shade with an occasional exposure to direct sun, and will grow in partial sunlight if it is well watered. It tolerates a range of humidity to be found in apartments and homes.

It can be propagated by cuttings in the spring.

Kenilworth ivy, *Cymbalaria muralis.*

Sometimes confused with *Linaria,* this is a species in its own right. The origin of its genus name is interesting. *Muralis* in Latin means "of walls." In England it is often found growing on old walls. The plant is a vine and roots easily at the nodes of the stems. The leaves are lobed and the flowers are pink, white and sometimes violet.

The plants can be started from seed in the spring, or by dividing older spreading plants.

nephythis, arrowhead vine, *Syngonium podophyllum.*

One of the more available house plants, popular because it can tolerate pretty rugged conditions and still hang in there and survice.

The plants are vine-like growing to 2 feet in height and can profitably use some support. Leaves are arrow- or heart-shaped, dull green, sometimes with silvery white centers.

The plants grow best in indirect light at a temperature no lower than 65°F. Holding water to a minimum will help keep the plant growing compactly, much to be desired in a plant that can grow rather rapidly. An occasional pruning will help it maintain a comfortable size.

Emerald green has dark green leaves with compact growth.

S. podophyllum xanthophilum known as green gold, has yellow green leaves with narrow green borders.

Norfolk Island pine, *Araucaria excelsa.* (Figure 56).

When we see a stately, symetrical Norfolk Island pine we think with pleasure of our many happy buffet dinners at the Faculty Club at North Carolina State University in Raleigh. Their handsome indoor garden had as its focal point a single Norfolk Island pine about 3 feet tall.

These trees are slow growers and beautifully adapted to low light and modest water supplies. The branches are borne in whorls around the trunk. The leaves are dark green and needle-like. The ideal temperature is about 65°F. in an area protected from drafts.

Home propagation is troublesome and the best sources are

Figure 56. Left to right: *Rhoeo discolor, Araucaria excelsa, Pilea caderi.* U.S.D.A.

commercial nurseries and florists. As with other plants if the tree becomes too tall it can be air-layered to make a new plant and the bottom discarded.

peperomia, *Peperomia* spp.

Another group of plants that can withstand pretty rough going. They tolerate low light, they respond enthusiastically to bright light, but direct sunlight in the summer should be avoided. Also avoid temperatures below 60°F. Variegated varieties display better coloration in bright light.

Propagation is by stem or leaf cuttings in the spring.

P. floridii has many stems and very small oval leaves (Figure 57).

P. fosteri is a creeping variety with dark green leaves and red stems.

P. grieseo argentea produces silvery colored rosettes with sunken purplish veins.

P. obtusifolia usually has fleshy green leaves; a variegated form has gold leaves with green markings.

P. sandersi, the watermelon peperomia, has its leaves in rosettes with red leaf stems. The leaves have silver stripes.

P. verschaffelti has broad silver bands between yellowish veins.

philodendron, *Philodendron* spp.

By far and away this evergreen is the most popular house plant group in the United States. Philodendrons are perfectly adapted to the variability of indoor living and survive under pretty rigorous conditions.

By preference they do best with bright light, but not direct sunlight, moist soil and a minimum temperature of 65°F. If conditions are rough for a prolonged period, such as water deficiency, pot-bound roots, low temperatures or poor drainage, the plant protests with yellow leaves and sometimes yellow spots.

If the plant gets "leggy" with age it can be cut back to a stub about 2 inches high and a new plant will arise. Aerial layering is possible, but we do not use this method with this plant. Propagation by cuttings, is common but not for all species, of

Figure 57. Left to right: *Crypthanthus zonatus, Peperomia floridii, Bromelia serra.*
U.S.D.A.

which there are dozens and dozens. We will only describe a
few.

P. bipinnatifidum, twin cut philodendron, has large, deeply
notched leaves.

P. dubium, cutleaf philodendron (Figure 58) has deep green
star-shaped leaves and is a slow grower.

P. oxycardium (P. cordatum), heartleaf philodendron, is the
most widely grown foliage plant. It has heart-shaped leaves, is
small and can be grown in water. It will survive with very little
light.

P. panduraeforme is the fiddleleaf philodendron (Figure 58).

P. pertusum, the Swiss cheese plant, is the young climbing
stage of *Monstera deliciosa* (Figure 58).

P. squamiforum, (Figure 59), anchorleaf philodendron has
leaf stalks that are covered with red and green hairs.

P. wendlandi and *P. selloum* can withstand very low temperatures. There are a number of red foliage types. The self heading,

Figure 58. Left to right: *Philodendron dubium, Philodendron pertusum, Philodendron panduraeforme.* U.S.D.A.

non-climbing species are not as well known because they require more room for their spreading manner of growth.

philea, *Pilea* spp.

There are several species of *Pilea* which make excellent house plants. There is some confusion in attaching the proper scientific name to the right plant but we have done our best.

Figure 59. Left to right: *Philodendron squamiferum, Schefflera actinophylla.* U.S.D.A.

These plants vary from small dwarfs to evergreens. They prefer moist soil, partial shade in the summer and full sun in winter with a minimum temperature of 60°F. Some drying between watering is recommended. Propagation is by cuttings which we have rooted in water.

When we lived in El Zamarino, Honduras, I kept a few of these pretty people in a shady corner of the orchid house.

P. cadierei, aluminum plant (Figure 56), has pretty silver markings on the dark green leaves and a quilted foliage.

P. involucrata, panamigo, South American friendship plant, is attractive for its compact, shrubby growth and its red-brown leaves. It is dwarf, reaching a height of 6 or 7 inches.

P. microphylla, artillery plant, has bright green leaves and flowers which discharge a cloud of pollen when shaken, giving birth to the name. This species requires clipping to encourage branching.

P. nummularifolia, creeping Charley, is suited for hanging baskets because of its creeping growth. It is dwarfed.

pittosporum, Australian laurel, Japanese pittosporum.

Pittosporum tobira. An evergreen with attractive, leathery gray-green leaves; *variegatum* is edged in white. The white flowers provide an added touch as they are quite fragrant and are particularly welcome since they bloom in winter.

The plants prefer bright light and moist soil and a temperature on the cool side, 55–60°F. It is propagated by cuttings.

podocarpus, maki, yew podocarpus, *Podocarpus marcrophylla.* (Figure 44).

Podocarpus is an upright evergreen shrub that does extremely well as a potted plant. It can be kept small by pruning. The leaves are up to 3 inches long, 1/3 of an inch wide, and are shiny above.

The plants grow in indirect sunlight with cool temperatures of 50–60°F., and low humidity. They can stand a lower temperature and some dryness quite well.

Seeds and cuttings are used for propagation.

prayer plant, banded maranta, *Maranta* spp.

The name of this native of Brazil is derived from the manner in which the leaves fold up at night. Its appeal lies in the interesting markings of the leaves. It is related to, and confused with, *Calathea.*

M. erythroneura, called the jungle plant, has red veins.

M. leuconeura kerchoveana has brown splotches on the upper leaf surface and red splotches below.

M. leuconerua massangeana has vivid foliage with bands of reddish-brown around a blue-green center above, and a purple color on the underside of the leaf.

The plants are best kept moist in a minimum temperature of 65°F., and in a range of light from the partial shade of a northern exposure to bright light.

New growth appears in February, at which time the old foliage should be cut out. The plants are propagated in the spring by division.

We have found a tendency to stem rotting if water gets into the crown.

purple waffle plant, *Hemigraphis exotica.* (Figure 60).

This plant is not very tall but can grow to fill a 6-inch pot by

Figure 60. *Hemigraphis exotica.* A. Krochmal

spreading. The oval leaves are wrinkled with purple veins or lines, thus the name purple waffle plant. It should have indirect sunlight and a temperature between 60–65°F. It should be allowed to dry out between waterings.

rubber plant, fig. *Ficus* spp.

Who is not familiar with that old standby, the rubber plant? Even produce departments of supermarkets commonly carry them.

There are several species adaptable to a wide range of growing conditions. In general these plants prefer a warm moist atmosphere, but they will do fairly well in the average home. They can be grown in shade or full sun. They do best in a temperature above 60°F. with a moist soil. Wipe the leaves with a damp cloth every so often.

F. elastica, rubber plant, is easy to grow and is probably the one most frequently seen in stores. It has large oval leaves that are dark green and leathery. There are several varieties, including variegated forms (Figure 48).

F. lyrata or *F. pandurata* (Figure 50). The fiddleleaf has thick shiny leaves shaped like a fiddle, a foot long.

F. pumila or *F. repens.* The creeping fig has small leaves and forms a mat.

F. radicans variegata is a showy variegated creeper.

schefflera, umbrella tree, *Schefflera actinophylla.* (Figure 59).

This large shrub or small tree has long stalked glossy green leaves that are divided into leaflets and spreads out like an umbrella. It tolerates the variable temperatures of the home. It should be allowed to nearly dry out between waterings although it may be watered heavily if quick growth is required. It prefers a warm room and low humidity.

screwpine, *Pandanus veitchii.* (Figure 61).

Our friend, Dr. Nancy Bower at the University of Auckland, New Zealand, is by far the most enthusiastic pandanus fan we know. She has told us much of its native habitat in New Guinea and its many uses, from food to fiber. The house variety can't quite make the grade for all these uses, but is attractive in itself.

The plant can grow quite tall to several feet in height. It has clumps of sword-shaped leaves arranged spirally along the trunk. The most commonly available form has spines along the leaf edges. A newer form, *P. baptisii,* lacks these spines.

The plant can survive unfavorable conditions but will lose its variegated coloring if the soil remains dry for too long a period of time. We allow the soil to dry slightly in between waterings. It prefers a minimum temperature of 65–70°F. We find that our plants are pretty adaptable and can be grown in indirect light as well as full sunlight.

Most of the plants produce suckers at the base. These suckers can be removed and potted to start new plants. As plants get older they sometimes develop bulky aerial roots which force the plant out of the container. When this happens we repot in a larger pot, pruning the lower roots at that time.

seersucker plant, *Geogenanthus undatus.*

This compact low-growing plant has dark green metallic leaves with gray bands and a red quilted underside. It should

Figure 61. Left to right: *Fatshedera japonica, Pandanus veitchii, Colliga elegans.* U.S.D.A.

be grown in moist soil in a warm place with a minimum temperature of 65°F.

snake plant, bowstring hemp, *Sansevieria* spp.

The nicest thing one can say about the snake plant is that it is almost indestructible. We had one in Raleigh that had lived for twenty-seven years in a bathroom window facing a shaftway that never saw sunlight. Year after year with an occasional watering it held its own.

Although it is a succulent, it is very popular and we include it here. The leaves are narrow, sometimes growing to 30 inches in height.

S. cylindrica has cylindrical grooved leaves.

S. laurentii has leaves with longitudinal yellow stripes.

S. trifasciata comes in several varieties, all in rosette form with color variations (Figure 48).

S. zeylanica has dark green leaves banded with light green.

Ideal temperatures range from 65–70°F. Propagation is by leaf cuttings and division.

spathe flower, spathiphylum, *Spathiphylum floribundum.*

A very hardy attractive evergreen with a beautiful white spathe (a spathe is an atypical or different leaf) that could readily have placed this plant in the flowering chapter. Blooming may occur twice a year. The flower stalk should be cut off after flowering is past.

It is hardy and will grow in poor light if the soil is kept moist and humidity high, by spraying if possible. A group of these plants is a prominent part of the garden display at the North Carolina State University Faculty Club at Raleigh.

A temperature of 65°F. is preferred but there is some leeway. Propagation is by division.

S. clevelandi is quite similar to *S. floribundum. S. manna loa* produces somewhat larger leaves and spathes.

spider plant, anthericum, *Chlorophytum capense (C. elatum).*

A running, trailing style of growth makes this graceful green and white striped plant excellent for hanging baskets. The slender leaves are long and pointed.

The plant will adapt to partial shade best of all, but will tolerate limited amounts of direct sunlight. It should be kept moist.

New offshoots which are readily produced can be easily propagated in soil or in water.

spindletree, *Euonymus* spp.

There are a number of attractive, variegated dwarf forms of spindletree available to brighten a room. The plants are hardy and prefer indirect sunlight, moist soil and a cool temperature of 50–60°F. at night.

Propagation is by stem cuttings but is difficult.

strawberry begonia, strawberry geranium, mother of thousands. *Saxifraga sarmentosa (Sekiba sarmentosa).*

This plant with many runners gets one of its names from the many young plants that it produces on the runners. Its other common names refer to the strawberry-colored edging of the leaves of the variety "tricolor." It is suitable for hanging baskets.

It prefers a cool location of about 55°F. and partial shade; the variety "tricolor" prefers a slightly drier soil and a little more humidity.

three-men-in-a-boat, purple spiderwort, Moses in the cradle.
 Rhoeo discolor (Figure 56).

Moses in the cradle produces a cluster of stiff lance-shaped leaves that are dark metallic green on top and purple underneath. Small white flowers appear in boat-shaped structures, thus the plant's name.

It will tolerate a range of light conditions, from sparse light to direct sunlight, but prefers partial shade. Moderate temperatures, 60–65°F., medium humidity and a moist soil complete the picture of this plants requirements.

ti plant, *Cordyline terminalis.*

These plants resemble *Dracaena* and are sometimes called that. They are tropical and many that we find in the United States are imported from Hawaii. We visited several nurseries on Oahu that produced ti plants for export.

The rather long pointed leaves come in a rainbow of colors. Some are green, others are red, purple, white, yellow, and some are spotted.

Propagated from stem cuttings, the plants prefer temperatures above 60°F., indirect sun to bright light though they will tolerate partial shade. A continuous level of soil moisture is needed.

velvet plant, *Gynura aurantiaca*

This is an upright species with fleshy green leaves almost covered with reddish purple hairs.

S. sarmentosa is a loosely twining species with lobed leaf margins. The flowers have an unpleasant smell and should be discarded before they open.

The plants like full sun, moist soil and a temperature above 60°F. Pinching the growing point will keep the plants compact.

wandering Jew, *Tradescantia fluminensis,* and *Zebrina pendula*

The spiderwort family Commelinaceae provides us with two plants with the same common name.

At Cornell University the botany department would have been hard pressed to function without the never-ending supply of *Zebrina* needed for cell studies. This prostrate plant has leaves that are purple below and green and white above. The fleshy stems root readily at the nodes or joints. When the plants are too long, make cuttings about 5 or 6 inches long at the stem tips and propagate them in water.

Zebrina likes warmth, a temperature of 70–75°F., moist soil and high humidity.

Tradescantia prefers shaded places, a temperature of 70–75°F. and high soil moisture. The leaves resemble *Zebrina* in shape but are yellow and white. It is propagated as *Zebrina.*

wax plant, wax flower, parlor plant, *Hoya carnosa.*

A vine featuring clusters of white flowers with pink star-like markings in the center. It usually blooms in the summer. As a climber it should have support; a small trellis or stakes will do.

The plant prefers bright light although it will grow in the indirect light of an east or west exposure. A minimum temperature of 60°F. is required although during the winter it can be kept at 50–55°F. Allow the soil to dry between waterings and reduce watering during the fall.

Propagation is by cutting anytime.

Chapter 7

FLOWERING PLANTS

Undoubtedly the most popular category of plants with the largest number of people are the attractive and sometimes fragrant flower bearers.

Their numbers are legion and include miniature roses and azaleas, geraniums, violets of all kinds, lilies and on and on. A favorite get-well gift or a housewarming gift is often a potted flowering plant. Some are annuals and die after blooming; others, with care, can be brought to bloom a second time or more.

Flowering plants require ample watering, more than do foliage plants and cacti, and frequent fertilizer applications. We find a mix of ½-teaspoon of 5–10–5 to a quart of water, used every three to six weeks during spring and summer, and sometimes early fall, keeps our plants flowering and healthy.

Flowering plants require a rich soil of ¼ sand, ½ soil and ¼ peat moss, and pots large enough to allow full root growth.

We think of our flowering plants as being mothers who need a little extra nourishment and room to expand in.

Some flowering plants require particular light conditions. These are given in the chapter on light as well as in this chapter.

achimenes, *Achimenes* spp.

Finely cut red or green leaves and red or blue petunia-shaped flowers bloom from May to August. The rhizomes, rootlike stem, are planted ½-inch deep from March to May, one to two rhizomes to a 6-inch pot. The plants require the full to partial sun of an east or west exposure with a temperature of 60–65°F. and prefer a moist soil. Flowers will last for several weeks if the plant is kept in a slightly cooler area. After flowering, water is reduced gradually so the plants dry up. The tops are then cut back to 1 inch, and rhizomes are stored over the winter in dry sand at a temperature of 45–50°F. Your refrigerator may serve the purpose.

African violet, *Saintpaulia* spp. (Figure 53).

African violets are by far the most popular flowering house plant today because they adapt beautifully to the average home. They produce single or double flowers, white, blue or red and blue combined.

Propagation is by dividing an older plant or by leaf cuttings. A standard potting mix, a night temperature of 65–70°F., and a slightly warmer day temperature of about 75°F. are ideal. If the night temperature goes below 60°F. flowering may be inhibited and in some cases the plant may die.

Avoid direct midday sunlight except from November to February, but provide good indirect light at all other times. Keep the soil moist by watering from the bottom. Wetting the leaves can cause discoloration.

If the leaf stems touch the rim of a clay pot, rotting may take place. If needed, use a strip of foil to prevent such contact. Wash the leaves with soapy water about once every four to six weeks, and let them dry in a shady place.

amaryllis, *Amaryllis* spp.

Tropical bulbs bearing a few large, attractive flowers, red, pink or white, resembling lilies. Leaves appear after the flowers.

Bulbs can be planted from November to February in a pot large enough to allow an inch or two between the bulb and the pot. Two thirds of the bulb should be buried in a rich mixture of peat, good fertile soil and dried manure.

Place the bulbs in full sun at a temperature of 65°F. plus or minus 5°F. and keep the soil moist. When the flower dies, keep watering the plant until the leaves turn yellow. Stop watering at that point and store the bulb in the coolest spot you have, above 35°F. When you want the bulb to grow again, resume watering.

When flowers appear we fertilize our plants about twice a month using 5-10-5, a teaspoon to a quart of water. When water is withheld, stop fertilizing. Bulbs should be repotted every second year. The bulbs can be used for many many years with care.

azalea, *Rhododendron* spp.

If you have an azalea you can, with care, encourage its flowering over a period of years.

These plants, partially because they produce so many flowers, require large amounts of water at all times and are helped by spraying the leaves about once or twice a week.

Beginning in the fall the plants prefer a cool temperature as low as 45-50°F. if at all possible. Some light is needed.

When the buds begin to expand and swell, remove the plant to a warmer location with a temperature close to 60°F. and increase the light. High moisture is essential during this period to keep the buds from dropping. A sunny window is ideal at this stage. Be sure to pinch back new growth during the spring until April or May when blooming will begin.

Azaleas grow in acid soils. A mixture of ¼ leaf mold and ¾ peat moss is good. If your tap water is hard, either use melted ice from the refrigerator or add about ⅛ teaspoon of alum to the soil surface once a month. Alternate a mixture of ¼ teaspoon of sulfate of ammonia in a quart of water with the usual 5-10-5 fertilizer at monthly intervals.

begonia, *Begonia* spp. (Figure 62).

Fibrous rooted begonias have succulent stems, shiny leaves and a continuous display of pink, scarlet or white flowers.

Tuberous begonias, with large, thick roots, and crisp, pointed leaves have yellow, white, orange or red flowers.

Fibrous rooted begonias are propagated easily by seeds and terminal cuttings. They enjoy full sunlight during the winter months and partial sun during the rest of the year. Warm temperatures, 65-70°F. are preferred, as well as regular waterings. Pinching back straggly growths will make the plant more compact.

Tuberous rooted begonias are propagated by tubers planted in March, with the hollow side up, and kept in full sunlight until May. If kept moist, at 65-70°F., they will thrive with less

Figure 62. Left to right: *Begonia semperflorens, Begonia rex, Begonia metallica.*
U.S.D.A.

light in an exposure with indirect light. Additional light from
10:00 p.m. to 2:00 a.m. during the winter will keep the plant
in bloom most of the year. Either a couple of recommended
fluorescent tubes or a 75-watt incandescent bulb 3 or 3½ feet
above the top of the plant will serve adequately. (See chapter 2.)

When the plants become too large, it is time to re-pot. Stop
watering the plants in September or October and let the tops
dry completely. About three or four weeks later remove the
tubers, cut the dried tops about an inch above the tubers, and
store them in a box of sand or vermiculite in a cool spot. Our
closets sometimes become crowded with such items.

calla lily, *Zantedeschia aethiopica.*

There are two kinds, one with white flowers, the other with
yellow. Both can be bought at flower shops and are easily
propagated from large rhizomes.

A rich potting soil of ½ soil and ½ peat is recommended. The
white lily is planted in August and the yellow in October or
November, one rhizome per 8-inch pot. The whites bloom in
December, the yellows in April.

They prefer a sunny area and plenty of moisture. The white
varieties prefer a night temperature of 55°F. and the white ones
60–65°F. When growth begins, move to a cooler temperature
at night. During summer reduce water application, then repot
the tuber in September.

Cape cowslip, *Lachenalia* spp.

These very small bulbs, native to South Africa, can be planted four or five to a 6-inch pot. Flowers may be red, blue, yellow and green.

The cowslip prefers a very rich soil mix of ½ peat moss, ¼ soil and ¼ sand. Bulbs are planted in August about ½-inch deep. Containers are then placed in a sunny spot and barely moistened until the green shoots appear. A night temperature of 45–55°F. is suggested. At that time gradually increase water application until flowering begins when water is reduced.

Blooming occurs usually in the spring. When flowering is over the bulbs can be air-dired and stored or allowed to dry and remain in the pots. In the fall, growth can be started again by watering.

Cape primrose, *Streptocarpus* spp. (Figure 53).

A small shrubby plant with small thick leaves and 2 inch long trumpet-shaped flowers with fringed edges in reds, blues, purple and combinations of white and purple. Blooming is a long term affair, almost continuous.

They can be propagated by seeds, offsets and leaf cuttings and their care parallels the program for African violets. They prefer moist soil in the summer and a decreased amount in the winter, subdued light, temperature around 60°F. and high humidity.

Christmas cactus, *Zygocactus truncatus.*

We find confusion existing as to which botanical division the Christmas cactus belongs to. A very similar plant, *Schlumbergera* has been called Christmas cactus.

Zygocactus, the true Christmas cactus, blooms from November to early January producing beautiful pink, purple, orange or white flowers at the end of the stems. The plants produce flat-stemmed fleshy branches which serve as leaves.

In early September the plant requires twelve hours of total darkness each night to encourage blooming. A dark part of the house or a cover of some sort are needed. The night temperature must be no higher than 70°F. for flowering.

The plants can be propagated from pieces of branches two or three segments long in a soil mix of ½ peat and ½ soil. Plant in the fall and keep well watered until the following fall when they should be allowed to dry out somewhat. They take full sunlight well.

chrysanthemum, *Chrysanthemum* spp. (Figure 63).

Available from the florist year round, they can be kept indoors but bloom only for two to four weeks around Easter. Plants with partially open buds are more desirable. They prefer a temperature of 60–70°F. with full sun. Keep moist at all times. A night temperature of 60–65°F. and direct sunlight during the day will prolong blooming. *C. anethifolium,* glaucous marguerite, and *C. frutescens,* marguerite or Paris daisy, may be propagated from cuttings taken from shoots in June. Paris daisy is coarser than the glaucous marguerite and has green leaves. Usually planted in a 6- or 7-inch pot.

cineraria, florists cineraria, *Senecio cruentus.*

The large flowers, 4 inches or more across, are showy and the plant is another flower shop favorite. These are difficult to start from seed and we recommend you not try it.

If someone gives you one of these plants, avoid placing it in

Figure 63. *Chrysanthemum* spp. A. Krochmal

direct sun, keep the soil very moist and if possible keep it at a temperature of 55–60°F. during the day and 45°F. at night. The plant is discarded after blooming.

There are two classes of cineraria, the *S. stellata,* which has smaller flowers and grows to 3 feet in height, and the dwarf with larger flowers and less height.

crossandra, *Crossandra* spp.

A perennial with dark green glossy leaves and spikes of salmon colored flowers which bloom most of the year. It flourishes in a moist soil high in humus and prefers full sunlight with east or west exposure. A day temperature of 70–80°F. alternating with a night temperature of about 65°F. is recommended. If grown at a temperature of 65–70°F. it will bloom for about six months after planting. The humidity should be kept high by an occasional spray bath and by keeping the pot over another container of damp soil or pebbles.

It can be propagated by seeds planted any time, or by cuttings which may take nine months to bloom. It should be fertilized weekly, using the standard formula. The plants were imported from India. In Jamaica, at Hope Gardens, there are lovely groups of Crossandras growing out of doors.

cyclamen, *Cyclamen* spp.

Most of the time cyclamen are bought at the flower shop as a potted plant, usually between Christmas and Easter, and already have buds and flowers.

They need lots of sunshine, and a cool night temperature of from 50–60°F.

Our watering schedules aim to keep the soil moist but not too wet and we avoid getting water into the crown of the plant. If the soil dries out, the plants will wilt.

When flowering has stopped in the late spring, let the plant dry by withholding water, then in June dig up the bulb, or corm, and replant in fresh soil of a mixture of ¼ sand, ¼ peat and ½ soil with half the tuber above ground and half below. With luck there will be plants sometime from December to February.

Fertilizer requirements call for ¼ teaspoon of 5–10–5 to a quart of water about once a month.

Easter lily, *Lilium longiflorum.*

These familiar gift plants with their handsome trumpet-shaped flowers are not well suited for long time house use and are usually discarded when blooming ends. To prolong the flowering period, bright light, moist soil and a night temperature of 60°F. is required.

If you have an outdoor area you can put the plant there during summer. After blooming, water the plant regularly until the foliage yellows. When frost danger is past, transplant to the garden. In the fall it may bloom again.

fairy rose, pygmy rose, *Rosa chinensis minima.*

These exquisite miniatures may grow to 8 inches in height and bloom heavily. However, most of us who grow them find it almost impossible to keep them going indoors for longer than eight or nine months. They simply need a period in the outdoors to survive.

If you can get them outdoors during the summer, bring them indoors in October and prune them to about one half their growth. Then reduce water in November and December and maintain them at 65–70°F. They may bloom again.

fuchsia, lady's slipper, *Fuchsia* spp. (Figures 64, 65).

This is our favorite flowering plant by far because of the vivid reds and purples of the flowers of many of the handsome hybrids.

It requires rich well drained soil, high in organic matter, and medium humidity. In September and October prune the plant heavily, leaving about four or five buds. For best blooming the plant needs a cool resting period during November and December around 45–50°F. and a bare minimum of water for survival and to prevent wilting.

In January, increase water and put the plant in a warmer place with a day temperature between 60–65°, and a lower night temperature between 50–55°F.

In early spring buds begin to appear at which time it is well to remove dead shoots. Any straggly shoots should be cut out as well to shape the plant. A slightly warmer temperature and increased light is suggested. At this stage of growth some of the shoot tips can be pinched back to keep growth compact. You may repot the plant now but we do not do this ourselves. Keep

Figure 64. Hybrid fuchsia variety "Dollar Princess." A. Krochmal

Figure 65. Hybrid fuchsia variety "Swingtime." A. Krochmal

the leaves moist by spraying or washing with lukewarm water two or three times a week. Blooming occurs in May or June.

Propagation is by means of shoots 4 to 6 inches in length, planted in sand and covered with a glass jar.

gardenia, *Gardenia* spp.

A few dwarf varieties are gaining favor among those who admire these flowers associated with the south.

Difficult to bring to flower indoors, they are a challenge indeed. They require full sun and a night temperature within a degree or two of 60°F. If the night temperature is much above 65°F. the buds turn brown and fail to flower. If the night temperature goes much below 60–62°F. the leaves turn yellow.

An acid soil, high in organic matter, a mixture of 1/5 leaf mold and 4/5 peat moss, full sun and medium humidity are required. Flowering occurs in the spring. Humidity can be maintained by spraying the foliage two or three times a week.

During spring a fertilizer mixture of a teaspoon of sulfate of ammonia to a half gallon of water is applied once a month, for two or three applications.

geranium, *Pelargonium* spp.

Geraniums do well in a range of light conditions from the direct sunlight of a southern exposure, to east or west exposures for a brief period of a week or so.

They can be propagated from cuttings in the spring and set in a mix of 1/3 sand, 1/3 peat moss and 1/3 soil in the shade. They do best with a modest amount of watering, cool temperatures between 55–60°F. at night and full sun. When watering avoid getting the leaves wet since they have a tendency to rot.

Plants which are repotted too often will fail to bloom properly. To encourage blooming during the summer we cut back the plant in early fall and reduce water during the winter. For winter blooming we reduce water during the summer months and keep the flower buds cut off until mid-October.

The most commonly grown species is *P. hortorum,* the zonal type, which produces single and double flowers and dark zones on the leaves. Blooming can range from four weeks to much longer.

P. peltatum is the ivy-leaved species, often trailing in growth, and usually with glossy leaves. If you get a trailing variety use it in a hanging pot.

Scented geraniums are in a class of their own. Their flowers are nothing to get excited about, the varying scents surely are. The citrus variety and the peppermint variety are two with scented leaves.

P. domesticum is the Lady Washington group, with flowers growing at the shoot apex. Dark, spotted pansy-like petals are characteristic. It usually flowers for four to six weeks.

gloxinia, *Sinningia speciosa.*

Gloxinia has withstood the test of time to rank high as a house plant. The large tube-shaped flowers may reach a diameter of 5 inches and appear in a variety of colors and color combinations.

Gloxinia can be propagated by seed, tubers and cuttings in the spring, using a mix of ½ peat and ½ soil. Seeds will produce flowers after about six months, cuttings about the same and tubers at four months. Blooming will continue for several months.

The plants prefer a warm night temperature of 65–70°F., moist soil and bright light but not direct sunlight after May 1.

When flowering ceases, keep the soil dry until the plant dries. Then store the tubers in a container of sand or peat at 50°F. in a closet or corner of the basement. If the tubers get dry, add a little moisture to the container.

In February or March pot in fresh soil; keep the soil damp, and grow in indirect sunlight at a temperature of 60°F. or as close as you can manage. Increase water applications as the plant develops.

impatiens, patience plant, *Impatiens sultanii*

These are probably a rival in popularity to the geraniums sold in flower shops. Easy to grow from seed, they can bloom within three or four months of planting in a range of colors from white to lavender.

They thrive in full sun, south or west exposure, prefer temperatures around 70°F., and drop their leaves below 65°F. Keep the soil moist and spray the leaves once or twice a week.

Pinching the plant tips in the spring keeps them compact and well branched.

lantana, *Lantana camera.*
Relatively easy to grow are these continuously blooming plants. The flowers are scented and vary in color from white to lavender.

They prefer full sunlight and temperatures from about 60–65°F., a moist soil and medium humidity.

They can be propagated by cuttings taken in April or May. If you remove flower buds as they appear until September the plants will be stronger and will bloom in December and January.

Seeds can be used for either early April or September bloom. April planting will flower in July and August, September plantings in January or February.

marigold, *Calendula* spp.
A small annual with stiff stems, dark green leaves and yellow to orange flowers. The seed is planted in rich soil in the spring ¼-inch deep. Then when 2 inches tall the plants are transplanted to 6-inch pots. Instead of transplanting, plant can be thinned out. It prefers full sunlight with medium humidity, adequate soil moisture and a night temperature of around 50°F. Discard the plant after it has finished blooming.

oleander, *Nerium oleander.*
When we lived in New Mexico we heard tales of home builders planting hedges of oleander, a poisonous plant to eat, to discourage roaming livestock from trampling lawns.

The plants are tall-growing with leathery leaves and white to purple flowers. They must be pruned heavily to keep them within manageable size.

A standard soil mixture of 1/3 sand, 1/3 soil and 1/3 peat has worked well with us. Although the plants survive with low water supply, they will flourish with a moist soil. Blooming begins in early summer and may continue all year.

Gradually reducing water from July through September will prepare the plants for over-winter storage in some cool spot. In mid-March watering can begin again and the plants will resume growth.

pocketbook plant, pouch flowers, *Calceolaria* spp.

Generally this is a florist plant with red to yellow flowers, best bought with buds and open blooms. It likes some sunlight, a night temperature of 50–55°F. and plenty of water. If the blooms are removed as they open, flowering will continue longer. The plant is an annual and will die after flowering.

If you propagate from seed sow in the early spring in a mix of ¼ soil, ½ peat and ¼ sand.

poinsettia, *Euphorbia pulcherrima*

On the campus of North Carolina State University, handsome red poinsettia plants are very visible right before Christmas, where the greenhouse plants reach the offices of various departments.

It is best to buy these plants from a reputable source because they do require a special routine of growth. They are sensitive to temperatures below 60°F., temperatures much above 75°F., sudden temperature changes and drafts. Some new varieties are out which were tailor-made by plant breeders to withstand variable house conditions. Cultural methods vary widely from expert to expert.

To carry a plant over for a second year of blooming you can try the following procedure, although it is work.

When flowering stops, about April, withhold water and store the plant in a cool ventilated area like a basement or a large closet. In May, cut the plant back to a point 6 inches above the soil level. Repot it in a rich soil mix, place in a sunny spot and resume watering.

As it warms up outdoors and night temperatures remain above 60°F., put the plant outdoors, if possible in partial sunlight. Pinch each shoot once as it reaches a length of 10 to 12 inches, until Labor Day. Then put the plant in a sunny spot, with a night temperature of 60–65°F.

Full darkness is essential for blooming, from sunset to dusk from October on, roughly from 5:00 p.m. to 8:00 p.m. It may be well to cover the plant during these periods with a black cloth bag.

primrose, *Primula* spp.

The familiar primrose is long-flowering during the winter, producing clusters of flowers in several colors. The plants prefer cool night temperatures in the range of 50–60°F., eastern or western exposure but not direct sunlight, and a steady supply of moisture.

Plants can be grown from seeds and cuttings but we prefer to buy started plants. If you want to grow your own we suggest seeds be used. Plant them about March or April in a mix of ½ soil and ½ peat and keep them at 60°F. in a cool shaded spot over the summer. In early fall increase the light gradually until about January when they can receive full sunlight. Blooming will begin about January or February and continue for several weeks.

One species, *P. obconia,* is reported to cause skin rash on people sensitive to it. It is a species that can be flowered a second season by reducing water over the spring and summer. In the fall it can be repotted in new soil. Other species are discarded after blooming.

rose of China, *Hibiscus rosa-sinensis.*

One of a large number of species of handsome tropical plants noted for their large flowers in a range of colors, borne during summer and fall.

Plants must be heavily pruned to keep them a manageable size and pinching back during the spring is one way of doing this.

These plants prefer a night temperature in the range of 60–65°F., bright light and moist soil. During blooming a weekly application of fertilizer of 1 teaspoon of 5–10–5 in a quart of water is recommended. When flowering comes to an end fertilize once a month.

During December, January and February plants should be kept at about 50°F. and watering reduced. About March, prune the plants heavily, reducing the size by one-third to one-half and repot in a rich mix of ½ soil, ¼ sand and ¼ peat. They should be watered well and kept in a warm sunny spot. During the summer a leaf spray of water will encourage vigor and blooming. Spraying twice a week will be adequate in most homes.

shamrock, *Oxalis* spp.

An attractive bulb which produces white, lilac or yellow

Figure 66. *Gerbera jamesoni.* A. Krochmal

flowers. The growth of the plant is drooping and useful for hanging baskets.

It is started by planting 4 or 5 bulbs in a 6-inch pot in September, in a soil mix of 1/3 peat, 1/3 soil and 1/3 sand.

Like other bulbs they are put into a cool dark place and watered lightly. When green shoots begin to force their way up move the plants gradually to brighter light until they are in full sunlight and increase water applications. A night temperature of 50–60°F. is preferred.

When flowering stops, reduce the water until the plants dry up, then store the bulbs. In the fall repot and begin the cycle again.

Transvaal daisy, Barberton daisy, *Gerbera jamesoni.* (Figure 66).

This hairy plant can grow to 1½ feet tall. The hairy leaves are 5–10 inches long and are lobed. The numerous pinkish or salmon colored petals are 3 inches long with a yellow center.

Chapter 8

FRUITING PLANTS

There are a number of miniature or dwarf fruiting plants that are worth growing in the home. Most of them require a good deal of light, plenty of moisture and high levels of fertilization.

We begin fertilizing ours in the early spring and monthly thereafter until fall, using a teaspoon of 5–10–5 in a quart of water and adding about a pint or more each time.

Fruiting plants do best in a rich soil mixture and our favorite is 1/3 sand, 1/3 good soil and 1/3 peat moss. All fruiting plants can be propagated by seed, except banana and pineapple.

Bananas are propagated by means of offshoots which appear around the base of the mother plant. Nurseries often sell potted dwarf plants which can survive and sometimes bear fruit.

Pineapples can be propagated at home very easily. These bromeliads may take twenty-four months to fruit but are handsome indeed. Simply cut the top off a fresh fruit, with its little rosette of leaves, and bury in the potting mixture with the bottom of the leaves about an inch above the surface of the soil. Water well and keep in a bright spot. This plant is a terrestrial bromeliad. A fertilizer program similar to the banana is suggested with the fertilizer being poured into the center of the plant when the leaves are large enough to form a "vase."

A favorite plant of ours is the avocado. It will not bear fruit in the home but if kept warm will produce a handsome dark green tree that will grow from 3 to 5 feet high. Much larger and it will need to be put out for adoption!

When we want an avocado tree we take a seed and soak it until the outer coating comes off. We then place three toothpicks into the seed, spaced apart around the sides. The seed is then placed in a glass container pointed end up, resting on the toothpicks, and water is added until it just touches the bottom of the seed. Keep the seed on a window sill, add sufficient water to keep the bottom moist, and in about a month or so a shoot and roots will appear.

When the container is filled with roots pot the plant in an 8- or 12-inch pot. Water frequently and keep in sun or partial shade.

An interesting and unusual house plant is the coffee tree. It is truly a coffee tree; we have had some bear a crop of bright red coffee cherries, each with two coffee beans. These are available at some nurseries, but we like to grow our own to remind us of our years in tropical America. The problem is to get green unroasted coffee beans. We buy what we want at a coffee store in New York. Two to four seeds are planted directly in a 4- to 6-inch pot in a rich soil mix and are watered regularly. Germination time varies with variety and age of the seed. When one seed has developed into a healthy plant with true leaves, we remove any others that have come up. Watering and fertilization are the same as for the other fruits.

Miniature peppers are propagated easily enough from seed. If you can get a few fruits you are in business.

Citrus is not best propagated from seeds as it does not come true and there is no telling what you may get. These are best bought from nurseries and flower shops, or through catalogues.

citrus, *Citrus* spp.

Meyer lemon, otaheite orange and calamondin orange are all popular as dwarf house plants. We have grown all of these and have made preserves from calamondin fruits from our own plant.

For fruiting, a temperature of 50–70°F. is desirable with direct to indirect light. Plants should be kept moist and have medium humidity. Regular potting soil used for other fruits will serve well. Fertilize every month during active growth with a solution of 1 tablespoon of ammonium sulfate to a gallon of water. Prune to keep the shrubs well shaped. Some varieties are grown from seed while others are better if propagated by grafting or cuttings. One grown from seed will often not produce fruit or will take many years to do so. The flowers must be cross pollinated to produce fruits by using a small brush to transfer pollen from one flower to the stigma of another.

Citrus meyeri, meyer lemon, dwarf Chinese lemon.

This spreading tree is almost dwarfed. It is grown for its sweet white to purple flowers and will bear a small number of lemons year round.

C. mitis, calamondin orange.

A very small tree with slender upright branches and leathery broad to oval leaves. It bears small fragrant white flowers that grow on the terminal ends of the twigs, and small yellow-orange fruits that are very sour but make fine marmalade. It usually bears in the winter from November to December.

C. taitensis, otaheite orange.

A dwarf tree with thin glossy leaves and a few spines. The fragrant white flowers appear in January but the golden orange fruit does not appear until Christmas.

Jerusalem cherry, *Solanum pseudo-capsicum.*

A 2-foot tall plant with deep green leaves, white flowers and round long-lasting cherry-like fruits appearing from October to March. The plant is readily grown from seed in full sunlight.

It needs a temperature of 50°F. or higher with medium humidity. Frequent water spraying will help. Keep the soil moist as dry soil will cause the fruit to drop. Fertilize regularly over the summer.

ornamental pepper plant, *Capsicum frutescens.*

This handsome specimen has small shiny green leaves and bright red and yellow miniature peppers. It prefers full sunlight with high humidity and a temperature of 50–60°F. It needs adequate moisture but shouldn't be moist or waterlogged.

It should be fertilized every two weeks during growth, especially during the flowering period with a solution of 1 teaspoon of 5-10-5 per quart of water. It should be set outdoors during the summer, then brought in and repotted in August. Pinch the tops back to shape, and to dwarf growth.

Chapter 9

CACTI AND SUCCULENTS

These look-alikes are sometimes hard to tell apart. All cacti are succulents, meaning they are fleshy, but not all succulents are cacti.

There is one very clear way of distinguishing one group from the other. *All* cacti have small areas or patches, called aeroles, which are the points of origin of bristles, spines and other such outgrowths, as well as the flowers. Use a hand lens, if needed, to examine your plant's surface to see if you can locate these soft cushiony patches.

Cactus flowers are usually large, colorful and borne singly. Many cacti have very fleshy stems which look like leaves and branches which bear spines or similar growths instead of leaves.

Growth conditions

Cacti thrive in the warm dry conditions of most homes, will go for long periods with minimum water and do not require much care. Most species need water not more than once a week at which time they are watered thoroughly. If they are watered too often the plants will rot.

A 1-inch layer of gravel or pieces of broken pot in the bottom of the pot provides good drainage and bottom watering is recommended. About September watering is gradually reduced to just enough to keep the plant from shriveling. In March watering is gradually increased.

Plants usually thrive in full sunlight during spring, summer and fall, but too high temperatures and very strong sun can result in sunburn. Less light is needed in winter during their resting period. Winter temperatures ranging from 40°F. to 60°F. are acceptable but the optimum would be slightly below 50°F. In March the temperature is increased. They prefer a high temperature in spring, summer and fall. Cacti prefer full sunlight.

Plants do not require fertilizer the first year, but beginning in the second year a solution of 1 teaspoon of 5–10–5 or 4–12–4 to a quart of water should be added once or twice a month in place of the periodic waterings, during spring, summer and early fall.

The best soil mixes should be high in sand to provide the drainage these plants require. We use 1/3–2/3 sand or sandy soil to 1/3 peat moss. A little limestone mixed in the soil, about a tablespoon per 6-inch pot, will keep the soil in proper chemical condition.

Bromeliads are succulents but form a very popular well-established group themselves. We list some of the bromeliads that are small enough for growing in the house at the end of this chapter after cacti.

Succulents

agave, *Agave* spp. (century plant).
Several species are small enough for growing in pots and can be kept small by fertilizing and watering at a minimum. They are propagated by plantlets produced on the flower stalk, by pieces of the offset or by seed.

A. filifera
Slow growing species with many branches growing to 2 feet in diameter. It has narrow shiny green leaves with white lines, is 10 inches long and 1 inch wide, gradually tapering to a point.

A. stricta, hedgehog agave
Spherical-shaped species with foot-long leaves 1/3-inch wide, tipped with a spine. The leaves are numerous and narrow.

A. victoriae-reginae
A slow-growing miniature century plant reaching only 6 inches in height, with a rosette of stiff thick dull green leaves

6 inches long and 2 inches wide, with sharp ends. The edges of the leaves have white lines that make it particularly beautiful. It requires more warmth than the others do.

aloe, *Aloe* spp.

Aloes vary from 3 inches in height to tree size but only the small ones are recommended.

Symmetrical clusters or rosettes of spiny pointed heavy leaves. The flowers appear in fall and winter and are pink, red, yellow or orange. The ends of the leaves blacken if the plant does not receive enough water. All prefer a dry house during the winter. They can be propagated from the suckers which should be removed and planted in the spring, or by seeds or offsets which are rooted, or by leaf cuttings.

A. aristata

Leaves are 3-4 inches long and ¼-½ inches wide.

A. ausana

Similar to *A. variegata* with leaves 5 inches long and up to 2 inches wide, arranged in a rosette of five to seven leaves.

A. brevifolia

This species has a short stem with a leaf rosette 3 inches wide, of gray-green lance-shaped leaves 3-4 inches long and 1 inch wide. The leaves have spiny margins.

A. ciliaris, climbing aloe

Stems ½ inch long and tapering thin green leaves 1¼ inches wide.

A. dichotoma, quivertree aloe

This species has stems and may begin to fork and become taller when it gets older. The gray leaves, arranged in a spiral, are 6-10 inches long and up to 3 inches wide. If the plant grows too tall it may have to be discarded.

A. saponaria

Has a short stem, and leaves 6-8 inches long and 2½ inches wide that taper toward the tip. The leaf edges have brown spines.

A. variegata, kanniedood aloe

A slow grower that reaches a foot in height. It has white marbled leaves.

Figure 67. Left to right: hedgehog cereus, *Echinoceraus* spp., carrionflower, *Staphelia* spp., prickly pear, *Opuntia* spp., barrel cactus, *Ferocactus,* spp., white torch cactus, *Trichocereus* spp. U.S.D.A.

A. virens
Green lance-shaped leaves are 8 inches long and 2 inches wide.

carrionflower, *Staphelia* spp. (Figure 67).
Fleshy 4-angled stems. It has large star-shaped flowers that grow at the base of the stem and can smell bad. It will grow in direct or indirect sunlight. Propagated by cuttings, division and seeds.

S. gigantea, giant staphelia
A sprawling plant with erect, 4-cornered stems growing to 8 inches in height. The yellow flowers can be a foot wide.

S. grandiflora
Dark, purplish-brown hairy flowers 6 inches wide.

S. hirsuta, shaggy staphelia.
Purple-brown flower with dense growth of 4-inch long hairs.

S. verrucosa.
Yellowish-red flowers 3 inches wide.

cobweb, *Sempervivum arachnoideum* (spiderweb houseleek).
Stems grow in a dense cluster or rosette and the tip of the leaves have soft hairs which give a cobweb appearance to the plant. It is very hardy.

crassula, *Crassula* spp. (jade plant).
Prefer lightest and airest part of the house and dry humidity in the winter. Older plants will produce flowers if grown in bright light and left a little dry. All except *C. falcata,* are good for growing on shelves.

C. arborescens, jade plant (Figure 68).
Dark green round shiny leaves. Can grow to 6 feet tall under good conditions.

C. argentea, jade plant.
Common, with sturdy limbs and a stout trunk. Bright green glossy leaves are thick and fleshy 1-2 inches long. The clustered pink flowers appear from November to April.

Figure 68. Left to right: crassula, *Crassula arborescens,* euphorbia, *Euphorbia* spp., kalanchoe, *Kalanchoe* spp. U.S.D.A.

C. falcata, scarlet paint brush.

It may reach 8 feet tall but usually grows to a foot tall with red flowers and thick grayish fleshy-shaped leaves.

C. lycopodioides, princess-pine

This irregularly branched plant grows to a foot in height. Each scale-like stem has 4 rows of tiny bright green leaves.

C. perforata, and *C. rupestris,* necklace vine.

It may grow from 1½-2 feet in height. Pale green leaves are jointed at the base and appear to be tied on the stem. Pale yellow flowers grow in spikes at the tips of the branches. *C. rupestris* is more prostrate than *C. perforata.*

cushion aloe, *Haworthia* spp.

A low-growing succulent with fleshy leaves that may grow in a rosette. The small greenish-white flowers grow in a long row. Partial shade in the summer, full sunlight in the winter. It propagates by seeds or offsets.

deer's tongue, *Gasteria* spp. (wart aloe).

The tongue-shaped hollow leaves grow in spirals, rosettes or rows. The tubular red flowers grow on long spikes. It prefers shade. It is usually propagated by offsets, leaf cuttings and seeds, although seeds do not produce true plants as we noted in the chapter on propagation.

euphorbia, *Euphorbia* spp. (Figure 68).

Some resemble cactus. The juice of some euphorbias is toxic and can cause dermititis. There are non-succulent and succulent kinds but we include only the succulents here. They may grow to tree and shrub size but only the small ones are intended for house plants. Propagation may be by seeds in the spring. Cuttings can be taken but the cut end should be allowed to dry before rooting. Plants should be kept moist.

E. caput-medusae, medusa's head.

A globular stem with snake-like twisted branches resembling medusa's snakes. The branches may grow to a foot long.

E. lactea, milkstripe euphorbia.

It has 3 angled stems and branches that grow to 2 inches in diameter. The sides of the spiny stems are flat with white and colored lines. It is a very slow grower but can eventually grow to be the size of a shrub or tree and may have to be discarded.

E. rugosa.

Stems 3 inches tall and 1 inch thick covered with spirals of thorn-like leaf cushions that are 4-sided.

E. splendens, dwarf crown of thorns.

Spiny, resembling cactus, with gray upright woody branches and round dark green leaves. Red flowers bloom during summer and fall. It will tolerate variable conditions. As it gets older it can be trimmed to encourage branching. It should have a temperature of 60°F. during the winter.

hen-and-chickens, *Echeveria glauca, E. secunda.*

Low clumps of stems with thick red bordered leaves growing in the form of a rosette. The flowers are red. Propagated by leaf cuttings and by young plantlets produced from the stem which can be cut off and rooted.

kalanchoe, *Kalanchoe* spp. (Figure 68).

These require more water than other succulents and should be kept moist. They prefer full sunlight during winter, spring and fall, partial shade during the summer.

K. blossfeldiana, kalanchoe

Dark green leaves tipped with red and bell-shaped flowers which appear in winter. Propagated from seeds or cuttings. If you want it to bloom for Christmas it should be kept in total darkness from 6:00 p.m. to 7:00 a.m. for thirty days beginning in September.

K. diagremontiana

It usually grows to 1½ feet in height but can reach 3 feet.

K. lanceolata, K. pilosa, panda plant

Blue-green fleshy toothed leaves are 3 inches long and form a rosette.

K. pinnata, good luck plant, life plant, miracle leaf.

This slow grower may eventually grow to 6 feet in height. It prefers light shade.

K. uniflora.

This is good for hanging containers. It has leaves 1 inch wide and up to 2 feet in length. The red flowers remain on the plant a long time.

K. verticillata.

Cylinder-shaped leaves arranged in a cluster at the top of the stem with the lower leaves drooping. It usually grows from 8 to 12 inches in height but may reach 3 feet with luck.

rosary plant, Ceropegia woodii, (string of hearts).

This viny prostrate plant has fleshy, heart-shaped leaves 3/4 inch long. Called rosary plant because of the circular growth along the stem, it has purple to pink flowers, is suited for hanging baskets and terrariums, and it will grow in full sunlight as well as partial shade. It is propagated by tubers.

stonecrop, *Sedum* spp. (live-forever).

Some of these grow to small erect shrubs while others are trailing. One of the best known is *S. morganianum,* the burro's tail, which has trailing stems a foot long. Others have fleshy or woody stems, all have small star-shaped flowers, either white, yellow or red. They are easy to grow. We collected many wild specimens in Greece and parts of the Middle East.

Cactus

ball cactus, *Notocactus* spp.
Usually globe-shaped but some are column-like. Covered with yellow spines. The flowers are of many colors and last for several days. Propagated by offsets and seeds.

N. apricus
Round flattened bodies and reddish yellow flowers 2 inches across.

N. haselbergii
Grows to an 8-inch wide, round body, with white spines and multitudes of red flowers an inch across.

N. leninghausii
Light green branching body growing to 16 inches in height. It does not flower until it is 6 to 8 inches tall, then it will bear 8-15 flowers a year. It prefers partial shade.

N. mammulosus, lemon ball.
Rounded green shiny bodies 3-4 inches tall with white spines ½-inch long. Lemon yellow flowers are 1½ inches across often borne in fours. It blooms in the summer at five to seven years old, it is easy to grow and will tolerate cooler temperature.

N. scopa, ball cactus.
Dark green body with white bristles and red spines growing in tufts or rosettes. Flowers are 2½ inches across and appear when plants are quite small.

barrel cactus, *Ferocactus* spp. (starfish flower), (Figure 67).
Globular or cylinder-shaped bodies the size of an orange. With ridges and colored spines. They are slow growers. Bell-shaped yellow-red flowers appear in the summer forming a circle around the top of the body.

Bridges crabcactus, *Schlumbergera bridgesii* (Christmas cactus).
The tubular flowers bloom around Christmas.

chin cactus, *Gymnocalycium* spp. (awlcactus).

Small round ribbed and grooved bodies resembling chins, thus the name. The large flowers are tubular. It is very hardy and will tolerate lower temperatures. There are about twenty-five species to choose from.

G. damsi, awlcactus

It only reaches 3 inches in diameter with pink flowers 1 inch across.

G. mihanovichii, striped chin cactus, plain cactus

It has pink, yellow or white flowers.

G. schickendantzi, awlcactus

It reaches 4 inches across and has 2 inch long white or pink flowers.

G. venturianum

A globular dark green body with tufts or spines. Blooms when quite small.

cob cactus, *Lobivia* spp.

Most grow in the form of large clumps and produce offsets. The flowers may be red, yellow or white. It prefers partial shade though it will grow in full sun.

L. aurea

Globe or cylinder-shaped stems are deeply grooved and grow to 4 inches in height. Large showy yellow flowers.

L. cinnabarina

A round to cylindrical body with dark brown spines and funnel-shaped red flowers 2 inches across.

L. hertrichiana, Hertrich's cob cactus

Small rounded stems that produce offsets and may reach 4 inches across but is usually closer to 2 inches. The 3-inch wide red flowers are abundant.

crown cactus, *Rebutia* spp.

These have rather flat round bodies covered with hair-like spines. They require more water than other cacti and should be shaded from the sun. The sandy soil should have added manure or leaf mold.

R. minuscula

Dwarf shiny dark green globe-shaped cactus made up of compact groups of 2 inch wide globular bodies. Has red flowers to 1½ inches wide along the base of the stem with up to a dozen blooming in April.

R. senilis

Overlapping round bodies growing to 3 inches in height, covered with long white hairs and spines 1¼ inches long. Rose-pink flowers bloom in the spring.

Easter cactus, *Schlumbergera gaertneri.*

Drooping branches with red flowers 3 inches long. It should be kept moist and fertilized frequently.

golden barrel cactus, *Echinocactus grusonii.*

May grow to four feet tall and 2½ feet wide over a good many years. Pale green ribbed bodies with spines in geometrically designed clusters and yellow and red flowers.

hedgehog cereus, *Echinocereus* spp. (Figure 67).

Usually cylinder shaped, low growing and prostrate. Propagated by seeds and cuttings.

E. pentalophus

Clusters of round narrow stems covered with spines and very large purple-red flowers.

moon cactus, *Eriocereus jusberi.*

Long, dark green, slender weak stems 2 inches thick with 4 to 6 ribs. The white and pink flowers 7 inches wide open in the evening and close in the morning. Plants should be kept warm in the winter.

night-blooming cereus, *Hylocereus* spp.

Triangular-shaped stems with aerial roots that cling to supports. The night-blooming tubular flowers are white to purple, red or greenish yellow. They prefer partial shade. A favorite is *H. undatus.*

H. undatus

This spreads to 4 feet in length with yellowish-green flowers a foot long. It produces red edible fruits.

old man cactus, *Cephalocereus senilis.*

Cylinder-shaped stems that grow to 2 feet in height. It is covered with shaggy white hair and should be brushed occasionally. Only the older plants bloom and the rose-colored flowers, 2½ inches long, open in the evening. It should have less water than the other cactus, even during the growing season. It should also have a warmer temperature in the winter.

old man of the Andes, *Oreocereus alsianus.*

It may grow to 3 feet in height and the 3-inch branches are covered with white matted hairs.

O. neocelsianus

Becomes covered with thick hair as it grows. *O. trolli* is another similar species.

orchid cactus, *Nopalxochia* spp.

Requires a higher humidity than the other cactus and indirect sunlight. Spray with water even during the winter on dry sunny days. It has stems growing on round or cylindrical bodies. The pink flowers bloom in large numbers.

N. phyllanthoides

Stems grow from thin cylinder-shaped bodies. Fragrant pink flowers.

orchid cactus, *Epiphyllum* spp.

Flowers are pink, red and purple appearing in April to June. It has long smooth flat stems with notched edges. Prefers the direct sunlight of a south exposure during the fall and winter, but an east or west exposure with partial shade is best during hot weather.

E. ackermannii, red orchid cactus

Grows to 3 feet tall with 8-inch wide red flowers.

E. copperi, yellow orchid cactus

White and yellow flowers 9 inches across.

E. strictum, white orchid cactus

Slow grower which may reach 6 feet in height in good circumstances. It has night-blooming flowers 6 inches long.

organ pipe cactus, *Lemiareocereus marginatus.*

It may grow to 25 feet tall over many years with many stems or branches resembling the pipes of an organ. If it grows too large the top can be cut off and rooted. It is also propagated from seed.

peanut cactus, *Chamaecereus sylvestrii.*

This fast grower has branches or clumps made up of cylinder-shaped peanut-like segments 2 inches long, green or brown with white spines. Produces 3-inch-long red flowers in spring or summer. It is propagated by rooting pieces of the stem, offsets or joints.

peyote, *Lophophora williamsii* (sacred mushroom).

Low growing with round blue-green or gray-green bodies 3 inches across, with tufts of white wool. Has a thick taproot and should be grown in a deep pot. White to pink flowers an inch wide. It is the source of the hallucenogenic peyote buttons.

pincushion cactus, *Mammillaria* spp.

Low growing and globe to cylinder shaped, single stemmed or grow in clusters. The small pink, red, white or yellow flowers grow in the form of a circle on the top of the plant. Club-shaped red fruits are produced. Spines vary in color from cream to white. It prefers full sunlight except in the summer when it should have partial shade. Propagated by cuttings and seeds.

M. bocasana, powder puff cactus

Round bodies 1½ inches in diameter growing in compact clusters. Covered with silky white hairs and brown hooked spines. Yellow and pink flowers are followed by long red seed pods in late summer that last for a month or longer.

M. camptotricha, birds nest cactus

It has 2-inch wide round bodies growing in clumps with 4-8 spines on each one and small green or white flowers.

M. carnea, blood mammillaria

Cylinder-shaped stems to 3½ inches in height with pink flowers 1 inch wide.

M. elongata, golden lace cactus
This fast grower has 4-inch long, cylinder-shaped bodies with small white flowers.

M. fragilis, thimble cactus
Short cylinder-shaped stems with a clustered globe on the top which can break off and be rooted. Each stem has 12-14 white spines.

M. hahniana, old lady cactus
Stem 4 inches high with red flowers. It becomes covered with white hair as it grows older.

M. heyderi, coral cactus
Keep moist in the growing season. It has cream-colored flowers that produce red berries.

M. kewensis, Kew mammillaria
A fast grower that reaches a foot in height with red to purple flowers and pink berries.

M. microhelia
This cylinder-shaped cactus grows to 6 inches in height with white down covering the top and white flowers one-half an inch long.

M. pabella "lanata"
Round and flattened with spines forming circles. One-half inch-wide flowers that appear when the plant is not more than 1½ inches across.

M. perbella, pincushion cactus
Light green body with spines. It is slow growing with several heads growing together to form one plant. Red or purple flowers. It needs little water, and then only when the weather is warm.

M. wildii, fish hook pincushion
Has round light green bodies growing in clusters and globe-like stems with hooked spines. One-half-inch wide white flowers.

prickly pear, *Opuntia* spp. (cholla, tuna), (Figure 67).
Can be dwarfed by growing in small pots in poor soil. However it is better to select the dwarf types, most of which will

grow in small flat containers, spreading and growing in clumps. If a richer soil is used they will need repotting every three years or so. There are two main types of opuntia; prickly pear with flat broad stems; cholla with cylinder-shaped stems.

The large showy flowers are yellow, orange or red.

O. papyracantha, paper spined opuntia

Flat oval joints with long white flexible papery spines 4 inches long.

O. ramousissima, holycross cholla

Shrubby branching with angled, slender woody stems. Begins to branch when quite small and resembles the famous sahuaro. Eventually may reach 6 feet in height. It has red spines and greenish-yellow flowers.

queen of the night, *Selenicereus macdonaldiae.*

A climber with light green, angled branched stems a one-half an inch thick, it climbs or trails with tiny scattered tufts of spines. The large, night-blooming, fragrant white flowers grow along the length of the stem up to 14 inches wide. It should be watered generously during the growing season. In winter it needs a warmer temperature than the other cactus. It is a fast grower, propagated by cuttings containing aerial roots. It should be trained when young to bend around large round canes fixed in the pots.

rat tail cactus, *Aporocactus flagelliformis.*

Trailing long slender flexible stems one-half an inch thick, covered with bristly hairs and hanging down from the joints. The red spring flowers are 3 inches long. It can be allowed to trail or can be trained on a support.

scarlet bugler, *Cleistocactus baumannii.*

Slender green to yellowish-green 1½-inch thick cylinder-shaped stems that grow to 14 inches in height. Branches only at the base. It is covered with long straw-colored needles. The 4 to 7 tubular orange-red flowers are 3 inches long and appear from midsummer to fall.

sea urchin cactus, *Echinopsis* spp. (Easter lily cactus).

Cylinder- and globe-shaped bodies with long tubular flowers

ranging from purple, pink to red and yellow. It should bloom for a long time in the summer if given frequent fertilizer. It can be propagated by offsets. It is very resistant to cold, should be kept moist and receive indirect sunlight.

E. eyriesii, hedgehog cactus
It takes two to three years to bloom if planted from seed.

E. multiplex, sea urchin cactus, Easter lily cactus
Dark green bodies grow to 6 inches in height with white spines in tufts. Pink flowers 69 inches wide.

silver torch, *Cleistocactus strausii.*
Small green cactus with erect stems, 2½-inches wide growing to 3 feet in height. Covered with pure white hairs and bristly white spines. It will grow in indirect light if necessary. The red-to-purple flowers are 3 to 4 inches long and tube-like, with tiny petals that open partially. Can withstand lower temperatures.

snake cactus, *Nyctocereus serpentinus.*
Long thin stems growing at maturity, fifteen years or more, to 8 feet with needle-like spines. Fragrant white flowers, 7 inches in length, open in the evening and close at noon the following day.

snowball cactus, *Espostoa lanata.*
May eventually grow to 15 feet in height but usually is much smaller. When young it is covered with white downy hairs.

star cactus, *Astrophytum* spp.
These are propagated by seed and should have a little more water than other cactus.

A. asterias, sand dollar, star cactus
Only 3 inches tall and 1 inch wide, it has flattened rounded segments. The yellow flowers are 1 inch long.

A. myriostigma, bishop's cap, bishop's hat
Globular body 2 inches tall divided into five ridges, brown wool and no spines. The yellow flowers bloom in the summer. It is covered with gray scales.

A. ornatum, star cactus
This slow grower will eventually reach a foot in height. The

3-inch wide yellow flowers appear even when the plant is quite small. Spines 1 inch long grow in clusters.

strawberry cactus, *Hamatocactus setispinus.*
Reaches 6 inches in height and produces yellow flowers and red cranberry-like fruit when only 2 inches in diameter.

white torch cactus, *Trichocereus spachianus,* (Figure 67).
A bright green cylinder-shaped body up to 3 feet in height with reddish or golden-brown spines. The white flowers are 6 inches across, fragrant and night-blooming. When it reaches a foot in height it begins to branch with erect stems. It is sometimes used as a base to graft other cactus on.

wooly torch cactus, *Cephalocereus palmeri.*
A tall-growing one covered with hair and deeply ribbed. It grows to 18 feet tall.

Bromeliads

Grown for their handsome foliage, some bromeliads produce beautiful showy flowers that may last a month or so. Others produce attractive berries. These are the most adaptable of foliage plants because they do well in the low humidity of most homes, in a range of light exposures from direct sunlight to shade. Many of them will survive without moisture in the soil if the vases, the central portion of the plant, are filled with water. Some are grown on blocks of tree ferns, a material available at flower shows and nursery stores, others may be potted.

They do well in direct sunlight. An east exposure is suitable during spring, summer and fall but a south or west exposure is fine in the winter. A warm temperature is helpful, 75–78°F. except in the winter when 60°F. is sufficient. Medium humidity is preferred. Spraying the plant with water occasionally is helpful. Water even less during the winter.

There are two major types of bromeliads. One grows on branches of trees and rocks, getting moisture and food from the rain and from the air. An example that comes to mind is the beautiful Spanish moss to be seen in the area around Charleston, South Carolina, among others. A second type called terrestrial, is found growing in the soil. When we lived in Honduras, the numbers and kinds of bromeliads found in the jungles and forests was beyond belief.

They are propagated by offshoots around the main plant after the main part flowers and withers or by cuttings taken from lateral shoots after flowering.

If you have an epiphytic bromeliad it can be propagated by fastening it carefully to an old piece of wood set in a suitable container; the roots can then be wrapped in spagnum moss in a manner similar to the air-layering technique we have mentioned in the chapter on propagation. About every four or five days the moss should be dampened. We use a plastic bag for this job.

If you have a land, or terrestrial, bromeliad it can be potted in a five or six-inch pot. The bottom inch or two is filled with gravel or pebbles for good drainage. The pot is then filled to the rim with a soil made up of ½ loam, ¼ soil and ¼ manure. Gently work the roots of the plant into the soil. Then gently add more soil, packing it into position. If the plant is tall, use some sort of pole to hold it in an upright position. Water, and if needed add more soil to fill any holes. Fertilizer on a monthly basis during the spring, summer and fall using one-half a teaspoon of 5–10–5 to a quart of water. We fill the "vase" with the solution.

A final word. Our favorite bromeliad, after wild Spanish moss, is the succulent and delicious pineapple.

airbroom, *Billbergia* spp.
Usually has leaves growing to form a sheath or tube with the showy blue, yellowish or red flower drooping down and growing from the center of the plant. The flowers are very short lived.

bromelia, *Bromelia* spp. (Figure 57).
These usually resemble pineapples, having lace-shaped leaves growing in the form of a rosette with spiny edges. Some grow to be quite large, as much as 6 feet across. So the smaller ones should be chosen. If propagates by stolons, stems just at or beneath the earth, which produce new plants from buds at their tips or nodes.

dyckia, *Dyckia* spp.

Stiff, lance-shaped fleshy leaves with spiny edges growing in the form of a rosette. The small yellow, orange or red flowers are tube shaped and grow on a tall spike. They range from one-half a foot to 5 feet in height. Smaller types should be chosen.

earth star, dwarf bromeliad, *Cryptanthus* spp. (Figure 57).

These bromeliads prefer indirect sunlight and are grown for their foliage and shapes. They have stiff leaves 1–2 inches wide with prickles on the edges and can be up to a foot long. The white summer flowers grow toward the center of the plant. They are allowed to rest over the winter in a cool dark place and are propagated by cuttings, offsets and stolons.

guzmania, *Guzmania* spp.

Leaves growing in a rosette from ½ to 3 feet in height can

Figure 69. Left: living vase plant, *Aechmea* spp. Center top: lobster claws, *Vrieria carinata*. Center bottom: earth star, *Cryptantus* spp. Right: neoregelia, *Neoregelia* spp. U.S.D.A.

be purplish, yellow, red or green. Flowers are cylindrical or tubular and are white or yellow.

living vase plant, *Aechmea* app. (Figure 69).
These come in two shapes, vase-shaped or tubular, and a rosette type. The leaves may be green-to-red or reddish-brown. The clusters of flowers vary from orange-red to pink-to-red.

lobster claws, *Vriesea carinata* (Figure 69).
This dainty plant has thin pale green leaves. Those closest to the yellow flowers are deep yellow with touches of red.

neoregelia, *Neoregelia* spp. (Figure 69).
Broad leaves growing in clusters, striped or barred above.

nidularium, *Nidularium* spp.
These have large sword-shaped or strap-shaped leaves that are prickly along the edges. Tube-like flowers are white, or red-to-purple.

Chapter 10

FERNS

Living as we do in western North Carolina near forested areas, and having spent several years in Kentucky in forested areas, we have a great liking for ferns which are found in many of these areas.

They make excellent house plants, offering a tremendously wide range of varieties to choose from to satisfy almost any preference.

Ferns require a very rich organic soil. A mix of ½ rich soil and ½ peat moss or humus is recommended. They like bright light but do not prosper well in direct sunlight. Moist soil, extra water during growth and a minimum temperature of 60°F. provide completely suitable growing conditions.

asparagus fern, *Asparagus sprengeri compactus*.

This is comfortably small, not over 18 inches tall. The berries are fragrant and a vivid red. *A. plumosus compactum* and *A. plumosus namus* are two dwarf varieties that ornament any room and can grow in hanging baskets neatly. These are not true ferns however.

birdsnest fern, *Asplenium nidus*.

A most eye-catching plant with stiff flaring fronds 2 to 4 feet tall, presenting the appearance of a bird's nest.

Boston fern, *Nephrolepsis exaltata Bostoniensis* (Figure 55).

One of the sword ferns, this is by far the favorite fern for

127

home growing. This variety is a mutation with large fronds that spread out. There are dwarf varieties too.

cretan brake, *Pteris cretica.*
Similar to the sword brake, but with slightly broader fronds. There are several varieties, one with white markings, another with different fronds.

green cliff brake, *Pellea viridis (Pteris viridis).*
The fronds of this plant are about a foot long with brown leaf stalks.

hare's foot fern, polypody golden wall fern, *Polypodium aureum.*
A fern that can grow too tall for comfort, but while young is very appealing. It has tall blue-gray fronds with gold-colored spores on the underside.

feather leaf fern, *Polystichum adiantiforme.*
This relative of the Tsus-sima holly-fern has leathery leaves 1 to 1½ feet in length.

maidenhair fern, *Adiantum wrightii.*
The fronds are 8 to 18 inches tall, the stalks are purple. This is a humidity-loving plant and must be sprayed every two or three days. *A. caudatum* has narrow fronds which trail. Small plants are produced at the tips of the fronds when they root on the ground.

mother spleenwort, *Asplenium bulbiferum.*
The fronds of this fern can grow to 4 feet in length under optimum conditions. This delightful plant gets its name from the habit it has of bearing borders of little plants on the upper surface of the fronds. There is a semi-dwarf variety, *A. bulbiferum laxum.*

tree fern, *Cibotium schiedei.*
In their native habitat in Mexico and Guatemala these handsome plants are found in jungle areas, often at high elevations. They can be grown in homes for a few years but get rather large eventually. The fronds may grow over 5 feet in length.

Tsus-sima holly-fern, *Polystichum tsus-sinense*.
An ideal plant for hanging baskets. The fronds may be slightly larger than 16 to 18 inches.

Chapter 11

PALMS

We love potted palms because they remind us of our life in the West Indies where a fresh coconut is a welcome to the visitor; of the date palms in Iran and Israel; of the unbelievably dignified walk lined with royal palms at the Escuela Agricola Panamerica in Honduras.

Most palms are not house plants by any stretch of the imagination. However, there are species that can be grown indoors.

House palms do well in bright light but do not tolerate direct sunlight. During summer they thrive on an abundance of water but reduced watering is recommended during the winter. A minimum temperature of 60°F. is needed but if light is very poor the temperature tolerance goes down to 50°F.

Propagation is by seed, generally a long drawn out procedure better suited for the nurseryman than the indoor gardener.

bamboo palm, *Chamaedora erumpens.*
Slow growing dwarf with several bamboo-like stems. It may grow to 5 feet in height.

Belmore palm, sentry palm, kentia, *Howea belmoreana.*
Tall and graceful with gracefully arching leaves rising at the top of the trunk. It can grow large, but like the others, this takes a goodly number of years.

Chinese fan palm, fountain palm, *Livistonia chinensis.*
The leaves form a fan borne on a short trunk.

fern palm, *Cycas circinalis*.

With fern-like leaves this palm may reach a height of 8 to 10 feet.

Madagascar palm, yellow palm, *Chrysalidocarpus lutescens*.

A feather palm often with a clump of slender trunks resembling a bamboo clump. It will outgrow your home ultimately. The spreading leaves are light green and yellow.

parlor palm, neanthe bella palm, *Collinia elegans,* (Figure 61). *(Chamaedorea elegans)*.

It may grow to 3 feet in height. A native of Mexico this palm is ideal for pot culture because of its dwarfed qualities. It can be kept for several years in a 6-inch pot.

pygmy Roebelin phoenix, *Phoenix roebelini* (Figure 55). *(P. boureiri)*.

It eventually reaches 6 feet in height but over a period of several years.

sago palm, *Cycas revuluta*.

This palm-like tree may reach 8 feet or slightly more in height. The leaves originate at the stem and spread somewhat like an umbrella.

sentry palm, kentia, *Howea forsteriana*.

Differs from the Belmore palm by having drooping leaves.

Weddell palm, Syagrus weddelliana (Cocos weddeliana).

This palm has feathery-like leaves and may grow to 2–3 feet tall.

Chapter 12

TERRARIUMS; GARDENING IN GLASS

The whole aim of this book is to help you bring some part of the outdoors into your home, to maintain touch with the green world of plants.

To transport an entire ecosystem, in miniature, into your home is one of the most satisfying and pleasing activities with plants that we know of. And that is what terrariums are all about.

When we lived in New Mexico and Arizona our home was filled with all sorts of small cacti growing in sand in a wide variety of glass containers, from nice neat aquarium-type tanks, to 1-gallon mayonnaise and pickle jars picked up at the university cafeteria and local restaurants. We usually left the tops off to avoid moisture build-up.

Sometimes a horned toad would be included if we stumbled across one in a desert field trip. If we had one, a screen went over his home.

Here in North Carolina we have found mosses and lichens our favorites, with an odd salamander included from time to time. We can, in our mind's eye, see and smell the forests from which we collected our small plants. Truly the out of doors has become part of our home.

Some of our friends, with great ingenuity, have established miniature Japanese gardens with ponds and polished stones, and tiny temples.

The only limit to what you can design for a terrarium is your own imagination.

Equipment

A glass container to permit passage of light and for visibility. Anything of glass with a top will do. If no top is available a piece of plastic wrap will serve (Figures 70, 71, 72).

Suitable soil mix. For desert scenes fine river sand is needed, or desert sand if you have a desert handy.

For a forest scene of mosses, lichens and ecologically similar plants, an organic soil mix is required. This can be found in the forest, if you are near one, or can be made by mixing ½ good soil and ½ humus, dried manure or peat moss.

Drainage. Pebbles, small rocks, charcoal, broken pots or even a mixture of these to include some twigs, leaves and the litter from the forest floor.

Plants. Just about any plant if it is small enough. If several plants are to be used, be sure they require the same growing conditions. Cactus and moss would be strange bedfellows. A list of some of the many suitable plants for glass gardening is given at the end of this chapter.

Preparation

Be sure the container is well cleaned, particularly if it has had food in it. If it is a food jar we remove the cardboard usually found in the lid.

First, lay down a layer of pebbles or other drainage material to prevent waterlogging of the plants. This layer would be 1 to 2 inches deep, depending on the container size.

Next, line the sides of the container (except for desert scenes) with 1-inch strips of moss found on flat stones and old logs, green side out.

Then place about 2 inches of your soil mix on top of the drainage materials. The mix you use will vary with experience but try to approximate the soil in which your plants usually grow. Slope the soil higher towards the back of the container to present a natural look and avoid a flat formal looking surface.

Very carefully place the plants in position with larger ones to the back so as not to block the smaller ones from view. Do not pack them in too closely and be sure they do not touch each other or the sides of the container, at least when they are first

Figure 70. An elegantly-shaped jar with its matching lid makes a beautiful forest scene for several ferns. A. Krochmal

Figure 72. A food jar makes an excellent terrarium for several small plants. The top is covered with plastic wrap. *A. Krochmal*

Figure 71. This brandy snifter makes a nice terrarium and has its own plastic lid. *U.S.D.A.*

planted. If the container is narrow-mouthed a pair of tweezers may be required to get the plants into position.

A few small rocks to resemble boulders, carefully placed between plants, will add a touch of beauty.

Once planting is complete, spray the plants lightly with water and then add water gently until the soil is wet, but not waterlogged. Clean the sides of the terrarium with a paper towel and cover.

Place the container in bright light but not in direct sunlight. Keep the soil moist as needed but be sure no water appears in the drainage material at the bottom. If this happens, remove the top for a few hours to permit evaporation. If small beads of moisture accumulate on the inside of the container your terrarium is in good shape. If the inside becomes misted, permit evaporation to get rid of the excess water.

Some Recommended Wild Plants

bloodroot, *Sanguinaria canadensis*
cinquefoil, *Potentilla* spp.
club moss, *Lycopodium clavatum*
  dogtooth violet, *Erythronium grandiflorum*
Dutchman's breeches, *Dicentra cucullaria*
evergreens, such as pines
ferns, small
goldthread, *Coptis* spp.
  jack in the pulpit, *Arisaema triphyllum* and related
    species
lichens, any
liverleaf, *Hepatica* spp.
mosses, any
partridgeberry, *Mitchella repens*
pipsissewa, *Chimaphila umbellata*
rattlesnake plantain, *Goodyera pubescens*
violet, *Viola* spp.
wild strawberry, *Fragaria virginiana*
wintergreen, *Gaultheria procumbens*

Some Recommended Cultivated Plants

African violet, *Saintpauli ionantha*
artillary plant, *Pilea. microphylla*

baby's tears, *Helxine* spp.
begonia, *Begonia foliosa, B. imperalis*
bilbergia, *Bilbergia nutans*
calathea, *Calathea illustris, C. rose-picta, C. zebrina*
*Chinese evergreen, Aglaonema commutatum, A.
costatum*
coleus, *Coleus* spp.
creeping fig, *Ficus punila*
croton, *Codiaeum* spp.
dracaena, *Dracaena godseffiana, D. goldieana, D.
sanderiana*
dumb cane, *Dieffenbachia seguine*
earth-star, *Crypthanthus bivittatus, C. zonatus*
English ivy, *Hedera helix*
fittonia, *Fittonia vershaffelti, F. vershaffelti var.
argyroneura*
flamingo flower, *Anthurium scherzerianum*
friendship plant, *Pilea involucrata*
gold-dust plant, *Aucuba japonica*
grape ivy, *Cissus rhombifolia*
Joseph's coat, *Amaranthus tricolor*
orchids, small
palms, small
peperomia, *Peperomia* spp.
philodendron, *Philodendron cordatum, P. micans*
pothos, *Scindapsus pictus* var. *argyraeus*
praper plant, *Maranta arundinacea* var. *variegata, M.
leucomerua* var. *kerchoveana*
selaginella, *Selaginella* spp.
snake plant, *Sansevieria* spp.
wandering Jew, *Tradescantia fluminesis, and Zebrina
pendula*

Chapter 13

FORCING BULBS

The advent of fall and cold weather is no reason to forego the pleasures that so many bulbs can provide indoors.

Bright colors, sometimes a soul-lifting fragrance, a forecast of the spring, are all at your command with a fairly simple technique.

A revival in bulb forcing at home, in schools and in offices is in full swing (Figure 73). Years ago when we were kids in school in the Bronx, we bought each spring for a few carefully hoarded cents, two or three narcissus bulbs to force at home. Bulb forcing is simply the method used to make them bloom indoors without than waiting for the spring.

Bulbs for forcing can be bought in the fall. We like to rush into the store as soon as bulbs arrive to be sure we get the best selection. We have found that we can get excellent bulbs from florists, nurseries and our favorite discount stores.

Select large healthy bulbs of the variety you have decided you want. Tulip bulbs should be over 1½ inches in diameter. This list will be of use.

Bulbs for forcing
Tender
>   amaryllis
>   narcissus
Hardy
>   crocus
>   daffodil

Figure 73.   This picture shows several kinds of bulbs being forced, and a variety of containers that can be used. *U.S.D.A.*

grape hyacinth
hyacinth
jonquil
snowdrops
Darwin tulips
early tulips
triumph tulips

If you get your bulbs before you are ready to plant them, they can be stored in a well ventilated location at 55–60°F. for several weeks. Planting may be done between October and December 1.

Containers

There are few limits as to the kind of containers you may use. As kids we were happy to borrow a soup bowl to hold our narcissus bulbs. The container should be shallow, not more than 6 to 8 inches deep. For paperwhite narcissus a container 3 inches deep is fine. For tulips, hyacinths and daffodils a depth of 6 inches is suitable.

Good drainage is as important for bulbs as it is for any other plant. Provide an inch of pebbles at the bottom of the container, or even better, a drainage hole.

Soil mixes and media

We recommend two mixes, No. 1 for hardy bulbs, and No. 2 for tender bulbs. The soil mix should come to ½ inch of the top of the pot.

No. 1 — 1/3 peat moss, 1/3 rich soil and 1/3 leaf mold
No. 2 — 2/3 rich soil and 1/3 sand

A third potting material can be made of inert materials such as pebbles, vermiculite or perlite (Figure 74). These are used for growing daffodils and paperwhite narcissus. Water can also serve as a growth media and is often used for forcing hyacinths.

Planting bulbs

Use only one kind of bulb for each container.
Plant hyacinths 3 or 4 to a 6-inch pot or one to a 4-inch pot, with the bulb tops showing above the soil.

Plant 3 tulip bulbs to a 5-inch container and 6 to 9 tulip bulbs to a 6-inch container, depending on bulb size. Place the flat side of the tulip bulb (Figure 75) against the side of the pot so that the lower limp leaf hangs over the edge of the pot.

Daffodils do best with 3- to a 6-inch pot, with half the bulb showing above the soil.

Crocuses, snowdrops and grape hyacinths are planted one inch below the soil surface with an inch or two between plants.

After planting water each pot until the water runs out of the bottom.

Storage

The planted pots should now go into a cool area where the temperature does not go above 50°F. If you have a cool basement this may be the answer. Burying the pots outdoors is another suitable way to handle the crucial period. If you live in an apartment and don't have too many containers, the refrigerator will serve very well indeed. When we lived in an apartment in Kentucky, one shelf was reserved in the fall for our bulb storage. We kept fruits out of the refrigerator at this time because many of them release ethylene, a gas that can hasten flowering. We used the next to the bottom shelf to be sure the bulbs did not freeze. Water the soil as needed.

The key to success here lies in getting the roots to develop without too much top development.

Forcing

The length of storage will never be less than ten weeks, and twelve weeks for large tulips, daffodils and iris.

When plants are removed from the refrigerator, yellow shoots should be showing. The plants should go into a partially shaded area with a temperature between 60°F. and 65°F. By all means avoid radiators, heat registers and warm rooms.

When the shoots begin to green up, gradually move the plants to brighter light intensity and a warmer temperature.

For a prolonged period of bloom, bulbs can be stored in and removed from the refrigerator at 2-4 week intervals.

Figure 74. Vermiculite (center) and pebbles (right) are two of the materials that may be used for forcing bulbs. Notice how the bulbs are placed in the pebbles in the bowl on the left. *U.S.D.A.*

Figure 75. These bulbs are being placed in the pot with the flat side of each bulb facing toward the outside of the pot. *U.S.D.A.*

Water culture

Hyacinths are often forced in water. Begin by buying a large bulb to assure a healthy bloom.

A French hyacinth glass jar can be bought readily. Place a bulb on the collar or rim (Figure 76) and fill with water to ¼ inch from the bottom of the bulb. Be sure the water does not touch the bulb.

Some shops sell pre-stored hyacinth bulbs which can save you a waiting period. Be sure to check! If your bloom fails to appear, cover the glass container with an ordinary paper cup until the bloom begins to grow out.

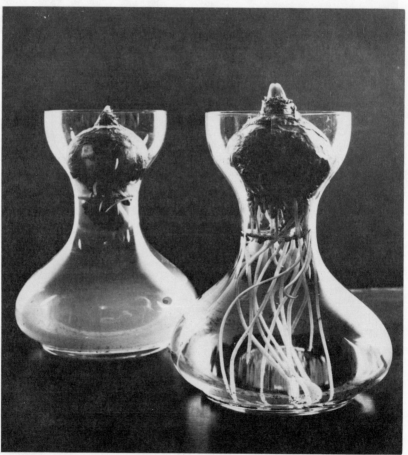

Figure 76. This glass container is especially made for forcing hyacinth. Notice the well formed roots with very little shoot growth. *U.S.D.A.*

Tender bulbs

Paperwhite narcissus

Paperwhite narcissus is by far and away our favorite bulb. When we lived in Afghanistan we enjoyed spring visits to the King's Garden where these sweet scented plants were grown with great care.

The yellow variety, Soleil d'Or, can be used as well as the white.

A shallow container 2 to 3 inches deep is suggested. It is filled to within ½ inch of the top with coarse sand, pebbles or gravel, and bulbs are set in the medium with their necks well exposed. Add water to ½ inch below the surface of the medium.

Place the container in a well lighted location with a temperature of 60°F. or slightly below. Be sure the water level remains where it was at the start.

At a temperature of 60-70°F. blooming will begin in six weeks. To delay blooming, the pot can be held at 50°F. and then moved to a higher temperature.

After flowering the bulbs can be thrown out, or reused. If you want to try to force the bulbs again, store them out of the container at about 45-50°F. for twelve to fourteen weeks. They can then be repotted and placed at 60°F. in bright light. Within four to five weeks you will have more blooms.

Hardy Bulbs

Amaryllis

Amaryllis is planted one bulb to a pot, with an inch of space around the bulb and half of the bulb above the soil line. Soil mix No. 2 is used.

Water well and set in a sunny location at a temperature of 60°F. or above. Flowering will begin six to eight weeks later. Keep watering the plants during his period of blooming.

After the flowers fade, cut the flower stalk off, continue watering, do some modest fertilizing and keep the plant in bright light.

When danger of frost damage is past you can place the plants outdoors if you have a spot or they can be kept indoors. Late in August when the leaves begin to turn brown, decrease watering. By this time the leaves are dead. Allow the medium to dry out, then store the bulb and pot at 40°F. to 45°F. In January repot the bulb and begin the forcing procedure again. Any newly developed little bulbs can either remain on the mother to help form a clump or can be removed with a part of the root. The little ones will bloom in two or three years.

Chapter 14

BONSAI

Bonsai are miniaturized trees and shrubs grown in pots, a technique we have imported from Japan. The basis for successful bonsai growing is the selection of those plants suited for indoor growth. Most bonsai require the out of doors most of the year and cannot be considered house plants. This is particularly true of forest trees. At the end of this chapter is a list, adapted from the United States Department of Agriculture, of some tropical and sub-tropical plants particularly suited for indoor bonsai gardening.

There are several ways of getting started in bonsai. One is to buy suitable plants from local nurseries or specialty houses.

Some indoor gardeners begin by collecting seed in the field, a bothersome process because seeds vary greatly in their germination requirements. We have bought kits, including seeds of apple and date palm and have grown these plants with a degree of success, until a move to another home set us back.

Others may collect small trees and plants in the wild, best done in the early spring before growth has begun. Such trees may be partially dwarfed already, due to the competition inherent in a wild plant ecosystem.

If you want to try your hand at collecting wild plants, an activity we enjoy in our family, we suggest collecting plants in an area under development for building or roads, *with permission* of the developer, usually given willingly. In other cases, collecting of trees and shrubs must be approved by the landowner. Remember, no collecting can be done in national parks, national forests, state parks and state forests. Be sure the material you collect is not on your state's list of protected plants.

We have spent some time collecting living plants in the forests of North Carolina, Kentucky and Tennessee and carry these plants in a back pack. You will need the following equipment:

(1) large plastic freezer bags or plastic sheets for wrapping roots
(2) plastic bottle of water (which gets heavier as you climb)
(3) G.I. folding shovel for digging up plants
(4) peat moss, dampened if practical
(5) string to wrap plastic in place
(6) pruning shears to trim roots and branches
(7) trowel to dig up smaller plants

When you dig, try to leave a good ball of soil around the roots. Remember that the distribution of roots in the soil is about equal to the spread of the branches above ground. When removing a plant, cut about half the root away with the shovel or trowel. Handle the roots, and particularly the taproot (the principal root) if one is present, with great care. We try to harvest plants less than 2 feet in height. Trim off any damaged shoots or roots with the shears. Then pack handfuls of the dampened spagnum moss around the roots and wrap them in the plastic bags, or plastic sheet. Keep the leaves damp with water from the plastic bottle to minimize plant moisture loss.

At home, carefully remove the plastic and plant the tree in a pot slightly smaller than the roots seem to require. A media of 1/3 sand, 1/3 soil and 1/3 peat moss seems generally adaptable. Very carefully straighten the roots when planting to help later on in the shaping. As the trees mature in their containers, part of the upper roots may be left exposed to give an old gnarled appearance.

Water the trees sparingly and use very little fertilizer if any. We have used a 2-2-2 fertilizer stick for about two weeks every three months. A year later, in the spring, move the tree carefully into a somewhat smaller container, trimming the roots back to about one half so as to enable the plant to fit. This procedure will be repeated once or twice more, repotting and pruning the roots by one half. At each repotting note carefully to see if the plants are pot-bound. The symptoms of this are the formation of a mat-like root growth. If this has happened, prune carefully to reduce by one half or so as we have noted.

Two or even three years after the plant has been collected it should be ready for the more technical bonsai training.

Plant qualities for bonsai use

There are two *objective* standards a tree should meet to serve as a sound bonsai. These are, small leaves or needles and a short distance between the point of origin of leaves.

There are also *subjective* requirements for a tree to qualify. A furrowed bark, or a bark that gives the impression of age even when very young, is one. Also, a tree that tapers towards the top is considered suitable for bonsai. Exposure of roots has been mentioned before.

The plan

An aesthetically attractive bonsai tree should be planned for when you begin. The trunk-to-be should be visible to the lower third of the tree. The branches should be "balanced," not geometrically, but sufficiently to present a pleasing design. The top branches should be smaller than those below.

Styles

There are five basic styles of bonsai, although all are subject to creative variations.

Formal upright (Figures 77a, b). This is probably the simplest for the beginner. The form is conical or mildly rounded at the top and the branches are horizontal. Often, a lower branch extends a little further than the others (Figure 77). The two lowest branches may be trained to come forward slightly, with a third branch projecting at the back of the tree.

Informal upright style (Figure 78). This differs from the formal upright in that the main trunk slants slightly to one side. You can achieve this effect by potting a young tree at an angle.

Slanting style (Figure 79). The trunk slants much more than in the previous styles. The lowest branches should spread in

Figure 77a. (top) This Chinese elm was trained in the formal upright style. *Longwood Gardens* **b.** (bottom) A mugho pine trained in the formal upright style. *U.S.D.A.*

Figure 78. This gingko was trained in the informal upright style. *Longwood Gardens.*

the direction oppostie to the trunk. The tree top may be slanted slightly towards the front.

Cascade style (Figure 80). The trunk begins to grow in an erect manner, then is trained down to reach a point below the bottom of the container. This style has the foliage growing below the soil surface. Low growing species are much easier to train than an erect tree.

Semi-cascade style (Figure 84). The change of growth direction is less abrupt than in the above. The foliage should not be allowed to grow below the bottom of the container.

Before selecting one of the five styles, study your specimen carefully to see which style will be most practical to develop. Try to visualize the plant in comparison to the illustrations in this chapter.

Figure 79.   A lodgepole pine trained in the slanting style. *U.S.D.A.*

Three operations are required to establish a finished bonsai: pruning, pinching and wiring.

Pruning

This is, by comparison to pinching, a large scale, major cutting out of unwanted foliage, and malformed and superfluous limbs. Remove crossing branches and dead branches and then carefully remove other branches until you begin to achieve the form you want.

Follow standard pruning procedures for sanitation, make pruning cuts above buds, and remove buds other than those on the outside of the tree.

Pinching

A relatively refined process of shaping a tree, used to remove new shoots before they become established. Pinching

Figure 80.   This pyracantha, or firethorn, was trained in the cascade style. *U.S.D.A.*

back new shoots will result in bushier growth. This can be done with the finger tips or a small sharp scissors. Any new or unwanted shoots or trunk and branches should be pinched back. Leave no stubs.

Pinching should accompany root pruning at repotting time, to maintain a balance between foliage and root system, and at other times as needed.

Wiring

This is the technique used to produce one of the final bonsai styles. Copper wires, sizes 10, 12, 14, 16 and 18 are commonly used, with 10 heavy and 18 light.

Figure 81. A yellow star jasmine trained in the semi-cascade style. *Longwood Gardens.*

Deciduous plants are best wired during the spring and summer; evergreen plants during winter.

Begin the wiring at the bottom of the plant, pushing the end of the wire into the soil and working up. The wire used is wrapped loosely in a series of spirals about ¼ inch apart. A thin pad can be placed under the wire to protect the trunk from damage.

When wiring is complete, the trunk and main branches are gently bent in the desired direction. The wire helps keep the plant in position. If a branch snaps off, cut it back to the nearest side branch; if it is partly broken, fasten it in place with a small piece of rubber tape as it may heal.

At the end of the year remove the wire from the tree, using great care not to snap the foliage.

Plants used for indoor bonsai:

acacia, *Acacia baileyana*
aralia, *Polyscias balfouriana, P. fruticosa, P. guilfoylei*
Arizona cypress, *Cupressus arizonica*
boxwood, *Buxus sempervirens*
California pepper tree, *Schinus molle*
camellia, *Camellia japonica,* and *C. sasanqua*
Cape jasmine, *Gardenia jasminoides, G. jasminoides
   radicans*
Chinese pistachio, *Pistacia chinensis*
citrus, (calamondin, kumquat, lemon, lime, orange,
   and tangerine) *Citrus* spp.
classic myrtle, *Myrtus communis*
common olive, *Oleo europea*
cork oak, *Quercus suber*
dwarf pomengranate, *Punica granatum nana*
elfin herb, *Cuphea hypssopifolia*
hibiscus, *Hibiscus roseo-sinensis* Cooperi
Indian laurel, *Ficus retusa*
indoor oak, *Nicodemia diversifolia*
jacaranda, *Jacaranda acutifolia*
jade plant, *Crassula* spp.
jasmine, *Jasminum parkeri*
miniature holly, *Malpigia coccigera*
mistletoe fig, *Ficus diversifolia*
Montera cypress, *Cupressus macrocarpa*
Natal plum, *Carissa grandiflora*
orange jasmine, *Murraea exotica*
orchid tree, *Bauhinia variegata*
powderpuff tree, *Calliandra surinamensis*
pyracantha, *Pyracantha* spp.
royal poinciana, *Delonix regia*
shower tree, *Cassia eremophila*
silk oak, *Grevillea robusta*
star jasmine, *Trachelospermum jasminoides*
Surinam cherry, *Eugenia uniflora*
West Indian cherry, Malpighia spp.
white popinac, *Leucaena glauca*

Chapter 15

VEGETABLE GROWING IN THE KITCHEN

Odd as it may seem you can grow modest amounts of a pretty wide selection of vegetables in an apartment if you have a location which gets some sunlight. A window sill, a balcony, or a doorstep protected from dogs. Fire escapes are, by law, out of bounds.

All you need to be in the indoor vegetable business is a suitable container, seed and synthetic soil mixture. Plants vary greatly in their growth requirements and we have listed the special requirements of many.

Containers

Just about anything that allows for drainage will serve the purpose. You can use flower pots, an old pail (Figure 82), a simple plastic freezer bag (Figure 83), an old plastic dish (Figure 84), a wooden bushel basket lined with plastic (Figure 85) or an old work bucket (Figure 86).

Be sure that you punch holes for drainage, usually 4 to 6¼ inch in diameter, along the bottom side.

The container you select as well as how many, will depend on how much space you have available. Six-inch pots are fine for chives. Radishes, onions and miniature tomatoes are suitable for growing in 10- to 12-inch pots. Large 5 gallon plastic containers are fine if you have a space large enough to hold them.

Figure 82. These white radishes are being grown in a plastic pail. Notice the drainage hole on the side of the pail. *U.S.D.A.*

Figure 83. Leaf lettuce being grown in a plastic bag. *U.S.D.A.*

Figure 84. This tomato plant is a variety called "Tiny Tim" and is being grown in a plastic pan. *U.S.D.A.*

Figure 85. Leaf lettuce being grown in a bushel basket lined with a plastic bag. *U.S.D.A.*

Figure 86. This pepper plant is being grown in a metal bucket. *U.S.D.A.*

Growth medium

The best soil substitute can be made by mixing this formula. It can be cut in half if need be, or increased.

¾ cubic foot package of shredded peat moss
equal quantity of vermiculite
½ cup ground limestone
¼ cup 20 percent superphosphate
½ cup 5–10–5

Add a little water and mix well. We use a garbage can with a tight fitting cover for this, to minimize inhaling the dust.

Seeds

Small packets are readily available in almost any grocery, garden store and discount store. I have never found an out-dated packet of seed and doubt that you will. This refers to the year stamped on the packet which tells you in which year the seed were meant to be grown.

Light requirements

Some vegetables need more sun than others. This will influence the kind you plant. If you have limited space with sunlight you will need to specialize in those vegetables that yield with less sunlight.

Some vegetables can be grown entirely in the house, using supplementary light sources. In this group fall radishes, leaf lettuce and the dwarf "Tiny Tim" tomato (Figure 84).

Planting date

If you are in the position of having some out of doors for this project, you will need to know the date of the last frost in the spring. This is only an average date which can fall earlier or later in a given year. We add seven days to the date. The local office of the National Climatic Center of the U. S. Department of Commerce, or the county agricultural extension agent, can tell you this date for your locality. The average date of first fall frost helps decide varieties to select, as some take longer to yield a crop than others.

Planting

If you start your plants four to eight weeks before last frost they will be ready to move to the exposed area you have in mind. You can start the plants in small pots, or in the peat discs described in the chapter on propagation. About two or three weeks after seeding, the plants to go outside should be hardened; that is done by reducing water and putting the plants in a cooler spot.

If you have a small number of plants set in an open area, they can possibly be brought indoors if a late frost moves in.

Water your plants each time the soil surface feels dry to the touch but avoid too much water. As the plants and the weather turns warmer, more water will be required.

Keep weeds out by pulling them up by hand. If you see any insects or diseases, use the appropriate dust recommended by your garden shop.

Table 1. Light adaptability of some vegetables

Partial shade	Full sunlight
beets	eggplant
cabbage	peppers
carrots	tomatoes
chives	
leek	
leaf lettuce (tolerates low temperatures)	
onions, green	
parsley	
radishes	

Chapter 16

PLANT PESTS*

by Dr. James Baker, Assistant Professor, Entomology Extension, North Carolina State University, Raleigh.

Even though you lavish fertilizer, proper lighting and water on your prize plants, something seems to be the matter! Upon closer inspection you notice that the foliage is pale and droops. Perhaps there is sticky substance on the leaves, and on the floor around the plant. As you turn a leaf over—egads, insects! But what kind? Two kinds of pests infest house plants, those with chewing mouth parts and those with sucking mouth parts. When you notice holes in the foliage or portions of the foliage missing, chewing pests are probably involved. (See the section on chewing pests below.) Sucking pests are more difficult to diagnose. However, many times honeydew, a sweet sticky substance, accompanies an infestation of sucking insects.

Sucking insects

Aphids are among the most common of the sucking insects found on house plants. These small, soft-bodied pests are often

---

*The use of trade names in this chapter does not imply endorsement by the author, or by North Carolina State University, of the products named, nor criticism of similar ones not mentioned.

found clustered along the stems and under the leaves of ornamental plants (Figure 87). Many times the honeydew excreted by the aphids is the most noticeable part of an aphid infestation. A black mold, called sooty mold, may grow in the honeydew and may cause the plant to become dark and unattractive. Aphids are sometimes difficult to control because they tend to wedge down into the crevices of a plant and thus are protected from a pesticide.

Scales are small insects which are protected by a waxy or lacquer-like secretion. There are many different kinds of scales. Scales feed by sucking sap from the stems and leaves of their host plant. Female scales lay their eggs under their protective cover, or scale, which protects the eggs (Figure 88). The newly hatched young scales are called crawlers because they crawl about the plant looking for a place to feed. Once the crawler has selected a suitable place it inserts its mouthpart into the plant and starts to feed. These insects are hard to control because of their scale covering. Two or three treatments may be necessary at seven- or ten-day intervals to control these pests.

Mealybugs are related to scales and aphids. Mealybugs have a soft, waxy bloom which covers their body giving them a mealy appearance (Figure 89). At first, mealybugs seem to hide on the plant and their presence is not noticed. Later, however, after the first mealybugs have laid eggs and the tiny mealybugs have hatched, the infestation becomes shockingly noticeable! The eggs are usually laid in a thick, cottony mass.

Figure 87. Aphids feeding in a cluster. *N. C. Agr. Ext. Ser.*

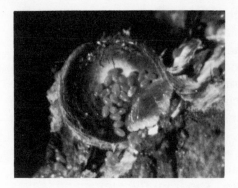

Figure 88. Scale insect with her protective covering raised to show her body and eggs underneath. *N. C. Agr. Ext. Ser.*

Figure 89. Mealy bug feeding on *Coleus. N. C. Agr. Ext. Ser.*

As each female produces a prodigious number of offspring mealybugs are difficult to control. The eggs enmeshed in the cottony mass are protected from pesticides. Also many of the individuals tend to wedge themselves into crevices on the plant and are untouched by the pesticide.

Whiteflies are those snow white, gnatlike insects which fly up from a plant when it is disturbed. Female whiteflies lay their eggs on the underside of the leaves. Tiny crawlers hatch from these eggs in a few days. The crawlers settle down and insert their mouth parts into the bottom of the leaf and begin feeding (Figure 90). It takes about three weeks for the whitefly larva to develop to a pupal stage. Whitefly adults emerge from the pupal stage within four or five days. The immature stages of the whitefly are very, very difficult to kill with ordinary pesticides. (However, house plant pesticides which contain pyrethrin, a plant product, are effective against the immature stages of whiteflies.) Like aphids, scales and mealy-

Figure 90. Whitefly adults on bottom of host plant leaf. *N. C. Agr. Ext. Ser.*

bugs, whiteflies excrete honeydew. Plants may become covered with the sticky substance. Sooty mold may also grow in the honeydew and ruin the appearance of the plant.

Thrips are small and slender, but they are not particularly cute. The blooms of white or light-colored flowers are often infested with thrips in the summer. Thrips wedge their way into the buds and feed on the petals with their rasping, sucking mouth parts before the blossoms open. After opening, the petals may appear brownish, distorted and unattractive. Thrips are not resistant to most pesticides but their small size makes them easily overlooked and often the damage is done before their presence is noticed.

Spider mites are not really insects but are more closely related to spiders. They suck out the contents of their host plant cells on the lower portion of the leaf causing tiny spots to appear on the leaves (Figure 91). Many times a thin web is noticed on the plant; hence the name spider mite. Spider mites lay their eggs on the leaves and stems of their host plant.

Figure 91.   Spider mite damage to a potted palm. *N. C. Agr. Ext. Ser.*

Within a few days, tiny larvae hatch from the eggs and begin to feed. Between each stage is a form called the resting stage or nymphochrysalis. The eggs and resting stages are exceedingly tolerant to pesticides. Therefore, when you treat for spider mites, repeat the pesticide application in seven days and perhaps follow up with a third application in another seven to ten days. Spider mites are small but they are visible with outstretched legs; an adult would approximately cover the period at the end of this sentence (Figure 92).

Cyclamen mites are much smaller than spider mites and are completely invisible to the unaided human eye. Their small size allows them to burrow into crevices and buds of house plants and to feed there long before the buds open. Their feeding causes tremendous distortion and the eventual death of the plant. Cyclamen mites are exceptionally sensitive to heat however and one may rid small plants of cyclamen mites by submerging the plant for fifteen minutes in water which has been heated to 110°F. Like spider mites, cyclamen mites lay

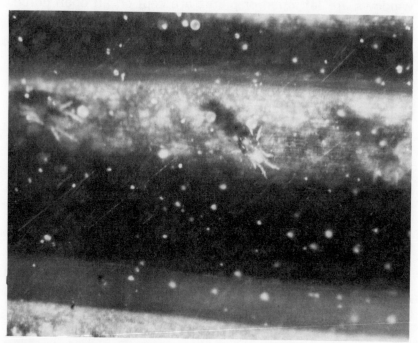

Figure 92. Spider mites and their eggs. Note the loose webbing. *N. C. Agr. Ext. Ser.*

eggs; however, there is only one immature stage, the larval. Cyclamen mites are fragile and, as mentioned before, sensitive to heat. However, because they burrow into the buds and crevices of a plant they are many times almost inaccessible to pesticides. A pesticide must be applied very, very thoroughly to rid a plant of these pests.

Chewing insects

Caterpillars are the inmature stages of moths and butterflies. Butterflies and moths usually lay their eggs directly on the host plant. The newly hatched caterpillars first eat their egg shell and then venture out on the plant, feeding upon the foliage or boring into the stem. Caterpillars are usually not a pest of house plants unless they are kept on an open porch or patio. Some caterpillars web the foliage together and hide within the webbed mass. Other caterpillars feed openly on the plant and can therefore be easily controlled either by picking off or spraying.

Grasshoppers are occasionally a pest of house plants if the windows are left open or plants are kept on an open porch. Adult grasshoppers fly onto the plant and feed on the edges of the foliage so that the foliage has a characteristic notched appearance (Figure 93). Grasshoppers are not difficult to control because they are large and conspicuous. They can easily be picked off or sprayed with a house plant pesticide.

Leaf miners, the inmature stages of flies and moths, are among the most difficult plant pests to control. The most common leaf miner pests of indoor house plants are leaf miner flies. The female flies deposit their eggs in the surface of the leaves and the young larval begins to feed on the tissue between the surfaces of the leaf. Feeding by the larvae makes a conspicuous visible tunnel which detracts from the appearance of the leaf (Figure 94). If the infestation is heavy enough, the plant will be damaged by the excessive number of tunnels. When treating for leaf miner pests of indoor house plants, using the pesticides recommended below, be sure and carry the plant outdoors when you spray it and allow the plant to remain outdoors until it is thoroughly dry.

Fungus gnats are an occasional pest on indoor house plants. The adult files look like miniature mosquitoes with dark wings

Figure 93. Grasshopper damage to *Bougnavillea. N. C. Agr. Ext. Ser.*

Figure 94. Leaf miner damage to chrysanthemum. *N. C. Agr. Ext. Ser.*

and no beak. The flies lay their eggs on the soil of house plants, and the tiny maggots begin feeding on the root hairs of the plants. As the maggots mature, they consume more and more roots. Finally, they work their way up the inside of the main stem of the plant, completely destroying it. Fungus gnat larvae pupate in the soil and soon new flies emerge to begin laying eggs around other plants.

When *snails* and *slugs* are found on indoor house plant pests, they have usually been carried in on the pot. Snails and slugs use their peculiar rasplike tongues to chew holes in the plant foliage. Females lay eggs. Soon, tiny slugs are merrily chewing away at your plant. Inspect the sides and bottom of any pots that are brought into the house to prevent infestation of snails and slugs. Disgustingly enough, hand picking is probably the best control.

Plant-associated pests

A number of indoor pests do not feed upon the plants themselves but are merely associated with the plants.

Ants, although arduous, are awfully aggravating. Ants usually do not feed upon ornamental plants; however their small mounds can be a nuisance and the fact that they many times feed on food which has been left out in the kitchen make ants an indoor pest. Because the nests of ants are sometimes found in house plants it is necessary to treat the soil of the house plant in order to control the ants.

Psocids are also called *barklice* and *booklice.* Psocids feed on a variety of dead organic matter but almost never on ornamental plants. Because psocids at times become numerous on the soil and pots of house plants, housewives become alarmed at their presence.

Sowbugs and *pillbugs* are often found around the bases of ornamental plants left on a porch or patio. At times sowbugs and pillbugs will feed on ornamental plants, but most of the time they merely feed on decaying organic matter and are therefore harmless. However, housewives occasionally become alarmed at the great numbers of roly-polies found around. These can be swept or vacuumed up and eliminated quickly. However, if a pesticide is applied it should be applied around the outside of the house in order to eliminate the sowbugs and pillbugs at their source rather than inside the house.

Control of house plant pests

Now that you know everything there is to know about house plant pests, controlling these pests is the only thing left to learn. Preventive, mechanical and chemical methods of control are names for doing-in these beasties inhabiting your plant growth.

Preventive control involves carefully inspecting every plant for pests before you buy it or bring it into the vicinity of your other prized plant possessions. Never buy a plant which is infested with any of the vicious pests for such plants will bring you grief! Friends who give you cuttings or plants which are lightly infested with an inconspicuous pest—are they really your friends or do you detect an evil glint of paranoic triumph in their eyes when you accept an infested plant? Preventing an infestation is much cheaper and easier than eliminating pests firmly entrenched on your plants!

Mechanical control (Figure 95) is a cheap, although time-consuming, method of eliminating pests. Hand picking or wiping the pests off must be done thoroughly. A cotton swab dipped in alcohol or fingernail polish remover is an effective tool for eliminating mealybugs, scales and aphids. Washing plants with a soft brush and gentle detergent will remove

Figure 95. Mechanical insect control. *N. C. Agr. Ext. Ser.*

sooty mold and aphids, spider mites and mealybugs. If the plants are sturdy enough, a stream of water will knock most of the insects and spider mites from the plants. However, always keep an eye on the plants in case of reinfestation.

Chemical control is a gratifying method of murdering those disgusting pests. Just spray a pesticide on and watch them fall off. However, pesticides can be dangerous when misused. A few commonsense rules should be followed for safe application:

1. Always store pesticides away from food or feed and under lock and key.

2. Do not let children or careless persons handle pesticide containers or apply pesticides.

3. Whenever possible, carry your plants outdoors to apply the pesticide. Wait until the plant is dry before returning it to the house (it is safe to handle the plants after the pesticides recommended below have dried).

4. Don't mix excessive amounts of pesticides. What little pesticide that is left over after treatment can be poured down the toilet.

5. Always follow the directions for safe use found on the label of whatever pesticide is used.

Malathion will control most sucking insects. You may have to use a small amount of household detergent to make the mixture spread properly on plants with waxy leaves (about ½ teaspoon per gallon of water). *Malathion* is sold as a dust, wettable powder or liquid. The 50 to 57 percent liquid is most suitable for use on house plants. Mix ½ teaspoon of *malathion* in one quart of water with a dash of detergent to make the correct concentration. This mixture can be sprayed on the plant or the plant can be dipped into the mixture. Remember! For good control, thorough application is essential. Even so, several applications of *malathion* may be necessary for whiteflies and mealybugs.

Sevin is a very good pesticide for control of chewing insects. *Sevin* comes formulated in so many concentrations that the least confusing thing to say is mix *Sevin* according to the directions on the label. *Sevin* will not control slugs, however. Use a prepared bait or mixture containing *metaldehyde* for slugs. The pot and bait should be placed out of the reach of pets and children, outdoors if possible.

Pyrethrins, a plant product, give a quick knock-down of insects. *Pyrethrins* are very safe to use and are very short lived in the environment. You may want to use a *pyrethrin aerosol* because of its safety and convenience. *Pyrethrins* are generally effective for whitefly. However, several applications at four or five day intervals may be necessary for complete control of whiteflies.

Chlordane is the pesticide to use for soil inhabiting insect pests. *Chlordane* is long lasting in the soil so that one good application is usually enough. *Chlordane* is usually formulated as a percent mixture and is mixed at a rate of 1½ teaspoons per quart.

A word of caution: *Use only pesticides labeled for application on plants. Many pesticides for flying and crawling insects are formulated with a refined kerosene solvent.* This kerosene will kill your plants!

Malathion, Sevin, metaldehyde, pyrethrins and *chlordane* are all avaliable at hardware stores, retail nurseries and garden shops and centers. Although it is cheaper per unit of volume to buy pesticides in the larger bottles, many times it is better to purchase the smallest package available. There are several reasons: In case of a broken bottle, the less pesticide spilled the better. Unless you have a tremendous number of infested house plants you will be surprised at how long a bottle of pesticide will last you. And pesticides do age with time; some lose their effectiveness in controling pests, and some may become more likely to clog your sprayer or to damage your plants.

Now the only thing left to do is to get up, grab your sprayer and kill those pests!

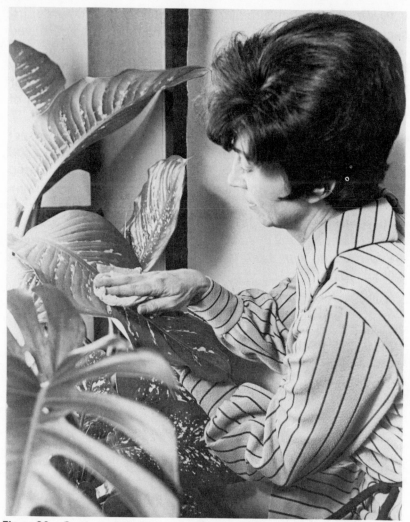

Figure 96.   Gently washing the leaves with a soft cloth and soapy water cleans them of dust and enhances their appearance. *U.S.D.A.*

Chapter 17

PLANT DISEASES

by Nanette Smith Henderson*

Though house plants are as susceptible to disease as garden plants, they are seldom infected because of cleanliness and sanitation practices followed by the indoor gardener that are impossible to apply outdoors. Likewise, house plants are rarely damaged by environmental conditions because we shelter them from snow, wind, sleet, hail and other potentially damaging elements. Gardeners find that it's much easier to protect plants from disease than it is to care for them, so let's discuss what precautions you can take to protect your plants from disease, and yourself from the work, expense and trouble of replacing sick specimens.

To help guard against disease and disease-causing factors it is useful to know a few basic biological facts. We should all become familiar with just what disease is. Very simply, disease is any condition that is not normal. Changes in the physical appearance of plants, such as leaf yellowing or browning, are keys to such situations and are called "symptoms." The occurrence of such symptoms can be caused by biotic or living factors, as well as by abiotic or non-living factors. A biotic factor may be a fungus, virus, bacterium or nematode (Figure 97). Abiotic factors would include such things as too much water, not enough fertilizer, cold and so on. The remainder of this chapter will be devoted to guidelines pointing out how to pre-

*Assistant Professor, Department of Plant Pathology, North Carolina State University at Raleigh.

Figure 97. Virus diseases are hard to identify, and impossible to treat. If you can diagnose a virus on your plant, it should be destroyed immediately. These are rose leaflets suffering from rose mosaic, a virus disease. *U.S.D.A.*

vent and, if necessary, treat the occurrence of biotic and abiotic disease-causing agents.

First is *careful shopping.* Always buy your house plants from a reliable dealer, one that will replace any diseased specimens free of charge. Also remember that plants bought from casual sources are sometimes inexpensive but may harbor disease-causing organisms that could not only destroy your

recently purchased plants but also could spread to and kill
more established plants. But if you can't resist a sale (I can't),
carry a small hand magnifier with you (purchased for about
50 cents) to get a really close look at the merchandise. Look
for any growth or markings that are not the same or characteristic coloring as the plant (this could be fungal or bacterial
growth). Of course, many organisms that may prove harmful
may still escape detection but I'd make the effort anyway.
Ask the salesperson about anything on the plant that does not
seem normal. Once you've carried your new plants home, keep
a watchful eye on them. Inspect them regularly for any disease
symptoms as given in the following paragraphs. Treat the
purchase and care of a house plant with the same concern
and care you might give a new kitten, puppy or any other
living thing.

Second, always do your best to *keep potting materials and
tools free of disease-causing organisms* (in other words, "biotic"
agents collectively known as "pathogens"). It is a good practice
if time allows to dust and repot all new arrivals. Leaves should
be dusted as often as your furniture, once or twice a month.
Dust reduces the amount of needed light that reaches the
leaf surface and can also trap disease-causing spores. Leaves
can be washed with a mild solution of soapy water (Figure
96) and a soft cloth. I just add a few squirts of liquid detergent to a pitcher of water. (Some house plant lovers swear
by skim milk, saying that it leaves a brighter shine.) A few
gentle strokes remove dust which might carry disease spores
and the leaves of your house plant will really shine! Fuzzy-
leaved plants, like African violets, can be dusted lightly with
a camel's hair brush. I use one of those brushes made especially for infants. I avoid artificial shiners in aerosol cans
because there is a great possibility of damage if they are used
incorrectly. Soap and water give leaves all the shine you could
possibly desire. My dracaenas especially, benefit from a good
bath once every month as do most glossy-leaved plants.

Third, if you put your house plants outside for the summer,
I'd strongly suggest that you *spray them with a general garden disinfectant* (fungicide, bacteriacide) *before bringing them
in for the winter.* It is quite possible that organisms which
remain low in number while exposed to outdoor weather con-

ditions might undergo a population boom once they are moved into a comfortable, warm, relatively humid home.

Fourth, remove diseased leaves, stems, and flowers as soon as they appear. Dying plant material can support the speedy growth of pathogens that can spread to healthy plant parts.

Last, be sure to keep plants as healthy as possible through *proper watering, fertilizing and light and temperature regulation.* Most house plant problems are a result of improper watering and over-fertilization. Just as people are more prone to illness when run down, so are house plants. A strong plant is less likely to become diseased than is a weak plant.

The above paragraphs constitute my preventive prescription. Do your best to follow this doctor's orders and I can predict, "Prognosis . . . excellent."

Of course, house plants can become diseased regardless of conscientious care. The following listings should help you to diagnose and, hopefully, to cure sick house plants.

Please *be sure to carefully follow directions on the containers* of all chemicals used*. The misuse of these compounds can sometimes cause you to experience very uncomfortable and unpleasant side effects.

There are quite a few problems and symptoms that can appear on just about any house plant. These signs are usually caused by the same abiotic or biotic agents regardless of what type of plant is affected.

Wilting is commonly caused by improper watering (too much or too little) or by the excessive use of fertilizer.
Rx: vary your watering schedule. I try to wait until the soil is "bone" dry before watering. It helps to poke your finger into the soil for about an inch to make certain that it's not just the surface soil that's dry.

Loss of Leaves. Sudden changes in temperature, lighting and/or ventilation could produce such symptoms. I've also read that unburned gas fumes can elicit such results from house plants. (See Chapter 1).

---

*The use of trade names in this chapter does not imply endorsement by the author or by North Carolina State University of the products named, nor criticism of similar ones not mentioned.

Rx: try moving the plant to a different part of the room or to a different room entirely.

Yellowing and Death of Lower Leaves. This can be seen especially on woody house plants such as dracaenas, rubber plants, palms, etc. Too little nitrogen or root crowding could be the culprit here.
Rx: try feeding your plant a fertilizer containing nitrogen and/ or transfer to a larger pot.

Overall Yellowing of Leaves. Soil moisture is usually too high in this instance. It's possible that this condition has already caused the roots of your plant to rot.
Rx: repot this plant, making sure that drainage is adequate. Reduce watering.

Leaves Look Small and Stunted. Open those curtains! Too little light most often induces this condition.
Rx: increase the amount of light available to this plant.

Brown Corky Scab on Undersides of Leaves. This symptom is most often seen in late winter. (Geraniums are especially susceptible.) Overwatering and/or improper ventilation are possible villains.
Rx: Reduce watering and provide better ventilation.

Browning Tips of Leaves. I always have this problem with my larger plants! The cause (or causes) is a difficult one to single out. Excess fertilizer, hot dry air and/or improper watering have been known to produce such symptoms.
Rx: experimentation and close observation are the treatments here. Move the plant around trying different locations while varying your watering habits. Good luck! You'll need it to unravel this problem!

Brown Spots, Yellow Margins and/or Tips On Leaves. African violets are especially vulnerable! Too much light affects most house plants this way.
Rx: reduce the amount of light or the intensity of light (i.e., move the plant from a southern to a western or northern exposure). Be especially wary and observant during late spring and summer.

White, Powdery Growth On Leaves, Buds, and Stems. What you're seeing here is the growth of a fungus. This problem is commonly referred to as "mildew." Sound familiar? The same thing can happen to your shower curtains or damp clothes. The cause of its appearance is the same in all instances: too much moisture (Figure 98).

rx: keep your plant foliage dry. You can try spraying with *Karathane* or *Benlate* (follow the directions printed on the container).

Death of Seedlings. This occurs quite often and is usually accompanied by a dark rot on the seedling stem at soil level. One or many fungi can cause this.

Rx: the best thing to do here is to discard all seedlings and start over. Next time pay closer attention to your sterilization procedure.

Figure 98. Mildews are common on all kinds of plants from house to farm. This shows powdery mildew on a rose leaf. Usually, powdery white masses appear on young shoots, leaves and buds. Distortion of leaves is visible in this photo. *U.S.D.A.*

Just about all of the symptoms mentioned above and in the rest of this chapter can also be induced by pathogenic micro-organisms as well as by abiotic factors. Since these organisms, i.e., viruses, bacteria, fungi and nematodes, are not easily seen it would be practically impossible for you to detect their presence before their damage to your house plants is visible. If all of my suggested treatments fail to cure the plant, it is quite possible that a biotic agent is present. In this instance I would recommend that you discard the diseased specimen and begin again, paying special attention to sterilization and potting procedures.

Certain diseases exist to which only specific indoor plants are susceptible. The following table is a general, though not by any means complete, listing of the symptoms and treatments for these damaging relationships.

Plant	Symptoms	Treatment
African violet	—bleached or tan spots leaves —leaves are crinkled and have a mosaic pattern of light and dark green areas	—keep foliage dry —discard sick plants
	—tan-colored fuzz and rot also appears on buds flowers and leaves	—provide better ventilation —keep foliage dry —spray with *Captan* (1½ tsp. to a quart of water)
	—black, slimy rot can affect stem, roots or crown of plants	—reduce watering —discarded infected plants —sterilize soil and container before reusing.
asparagus fern	—leaves turn brown, winter and fall	—lower room temperature, 70–72°F.
begonia	—large, round swellings on stem —tan-colored fuzz and rot	—discard infected plants (see African violets)
cactus	—corky, rust-colored spots, plants may fail to flower	—increase light —decrease humidity
caladium	—soft, mushy rotting tuber	—discard infected bulbs and check to be sure new bulbs are healthy (reputable businesses will guarantee their plant material)

Plant	Symptoms	Treatment
English ivy	—spots on stems are mushy and light green. Spots turn brown or black with a red margin.	—water plants from below
fern	—swollen areas or knots on leaves	—galls are not a sign of disease but are a natural part of this plant
gardenia	—discolored, sunken areas on stem at soil level. Leaves wilt, yellow and fall.	—reduce water and improve drainage
	—bleached, yellow leaves with green veins. Entire plant looks weak.	—treat with *Sequestrene* (follow directions on label)
	—buds fall from plants before opening	—raise temperature and avoid sudden temperature changes —keep humidity high
geranium	—discolored areas or spots appear on leaves of plant	—pick off and destroy affected leaves
	—black, slimy rot on leaves etc.	—see African violets
German ivy	—foliage is covered with mold and dies	—reduce humidity by spacing plants further apart —spray with *Zineb*
peperomia	—light, green rings appear on leaves	—repot
	—plants are stunted and distorted	—discard infected plants
	—black, slimy rot on leaves etc.	—see African violet
philodendron (also affects	—dead regions on leaves	—avoid too low temperatures —keep foliage dry
Chinese evergreen, dumb cane)	—leaves have brown spots	—spray with *Zineb*

Plant	Symptoms	Treatment
poinsettia	—leaves turn yellow and fall	—refer also to general diseases —expose to warmer temperature —increase light
	—black, slimy rot etc.	—see African violet
rubber plant	—bleached or tan spots on leaves	—move to lower light intensity —increase humidity
	—spots of dead tissue will dry up and fall out	—spray with *Zineb* (1½ tsp. to a quart of water)

Bibliography

GENERAL

California Agricultural Extension Service. *Care of House Plants.* OSA-#49, University of California, Berkeley, California.

Indiana Coperative Extension Service. *House Plants.* HO-56, Purdue University, Lafayette, Indiana.

Minnesota Agricultural Extension Service. *Care of House Plants.* Ext. Bulletin 274, University of Minnesota, 1970, St. Paul, Minnesota.

New Jersey Cooperative Extension Service. *Care of House Plants.* Ext. Bulletin 337-A, College of Agriculture and Environmental Science, Rutgers University-the State University of New Jersey, New Brunswick, New Jersey.

North Carolina Agricultural Extension Service. *Culture of Plants in the Home.* Horticultural Information Leaflet No. 410, Horticultural Science Department, North Carolina State University, October 1965, Raleigh, N.C.

Pennsylvania Extension Service. *Care of Holiday Plants.* Circular 549, The Pennsylvania State University, College of Agriculture, University Park, Pa.

U. S. Department of Agriculture. *Selecting and Growing House Plants.* Home and Garden Bulletin No. 82, April 1968, Washington, D.C.

——, *The Yearbook of Agriculture "Landscape for Living."* 1972, Washington, D.C.

LIGHTING

New York Cooperative Extension Service. *Artificial Lighting for Decorative Plants*. Bulletin 1087, New York State College of Agriculture and Life Science, Cornell University, September 1972, Ithaca, New York.

U. S. Department of Agriculture. *Indoor Gardens with Controlled Lighting*. Home and Garden Bulletin No. 187, May 1971, Washington, D.C.

Virginia Agricultural Extension Division. *How Plants Grow Under Light*. Publication 381, Virginia Polytechnic Institute and State University, July 1970, Blacksburg, Va.

PROPAGATION

California Agricultural Extension Service. *Mist Propagation of Plants at Home*. No. OSA-#184, University of California, Berkeley, California.

——, *Small Scale Plant Propagation Units*. OSA-#185, University of California, December 1966, Berkeley, California.

Illinois Cooperative Extension Service. *Plant Regulators Their Use as a Hobby*. Circular 886, University of Illinois, 1973, Urbana-Champaign, Illinois.

——, *Germinating Flower Seeds*. Circular 1077, University of Illinois, March 1973, Urbana-Champaign, Illinois

New York Cooperative Extension Service. *Propagation of Plants by Cuttings in the Home*. No. H131, Department of Floriculture and Ornamental Horticulture, College of Agriculture, Cornell University, Ithaca, New York.

——, *Propagation of House Plants*. Extension Bulletin 1086, College of Agriculture, Cornell University, Ithaca, N. Y.

——, *Flowers from Seed*. Information Bulletin 20, College of Agriculture and Life Sciences, Cornell University, August 1971, Ithaca, N.Y.

Pennsylvania Extension Service. *Propagating House Plants.* The Pennsylvania State University, College of Agriculture, University Park, Pa.

U. S. Department of Agriculture. *Windowsill Greenhouse.* Picture Story No. 190, Agricultural Research Service, November 1965, Washington, D.C.

Virginia Cooperative Extension Division. *Transplanting of Seedlings.* Publication 65, Virginia Polytechnic Institute and State University, September 1972, Blacksburg, Virginia.

——, *Propagation by Cuttings.* Publication 75, Virginia Polytechnic Institute and State University, May 1973, Blacksburg, Virginia.

FOLIAGE

Connecticut Cooperative Extension Service. *Cultural Pointers for Wax Plants, Hoya carnosa.* No. 65-46, College of Agriculture, The University of Connecticut, 1965, Storrs, Connecticut.

New Jersey Cooperative Extension Service. *Foliage Plants for Interiors.* Extension Bulletin 327-A, College of Agriculture and Environmental Science, Rutgers-the State University, New Brunswick, New Jersey.

North Carolina Agricultural Extension Service. *Growing Caladiums.* Horticultural Science Department, Horticultural Information Leaflet No. 525, North Carolina State University, November 1971, Raleigh, N.C.

FLOWERING

Connecticut Cooperative Extension Service. *Forcing Shrubs Indoors.* No. 65-45, College of Agriculture, the University of Connecticut, July 1967, Storrs, Connecticut.

——, *Geraniums at Home.* No. 68-27, College of Agriculture, the University of Connecticut, July 1968, Storrs, Connecticut.

Illinois Cooperative Extension Service, *Flowering Gift Plants. —Their Care and How to Rebloom Them.* Circular 801, College of Agriculture, University of Illinois at Urbana-Champaign, October 1970, Urbana-Champaign, Illinois.

——, *Geraniums for the Home and Garden.* Circular 904, College of Agriculture, University of Illinois at Urbana-Champaign, Urbana-Champaign, Illinois.

New Jersey Cooperative Extension Service. *Growing Caladiums as House Plants.* Circular 530, College of Agriculture and Environmental Science, Rutgers University—the State University of New Jersey, New Brunswick, N.J.

New York Cooperative Extension Service. *Geranium Culture.* No. CCF-162, Department of Floriculture and Ornamental Horticulture, College of Agriculture, Cornell University, Ithaca, N.Y.

——, *Poinsettas in the Home.* Department of Floriculture and Ornamental Horticulture, College of Agriculture, Cornell University, Ithaca, N.Y.

Virginia Cooperative Extension Service, *Home Care of Poinsettas.* Publication No. 375, Virginia Polytechnic Institute and State University, July 1970, Blacksburg, Virginia.

——, *Chrysanthemum for the Home.* Publication 382, Virginia Polytechnic Institute and State University, March 1970, Blacksburg, Virginia.

——, *Geraniums for the Home.* Publication 383, Virginia Polytechnic Institute and State University, July 1970, Blacksburg, Virginia.

Wisconsin Cooperative Extension Service. *How to Grow African Violets.* Circular 437, University of Wisconsin, July 1968, St. Paul, Minnesota.

FRUITING

Connecticut Cooperative Extension Service. *Cultural Pointers for Avocadoes and Citrus as House Plants.* No. 65-29, University of Connecticut, July 1965, Storrs, Connecticut.

CACTUS

Connecticut Cooperative Extension Service. *Cultural Pointers for Cacti.* No. 65-44. College of Agriculture and Natural Resources, the University of Connecticut, February 1973, Storrs, Connecticut.

New York Cooperative Extension Service. *Cultural Information for Cacti.* Department of Ornamental Horticulture, College of Agriculture, Cornell University, January 1962, Ithaca, New York.

TERRARIUMS

New York Cooperative Extension Service. *How to Make a Terrarium.* Extension Bulletin 1029, College of Agriculture and Life Sciences, Cornell University, May 1973, Ithaca, New York.

Virginia Cooperative Extension Service. *Terrariums.* Publication 40, Virginia Polytechnic Institute and tate University, May 1973, Blacksburg, Va.

FORCING BULBS

Indiana Cooperative Extension Service. *Forcing Bulbs for Indoor Bloom.* HO-19, Purdue University, West Lafayette, Indiana.

New York Cooperative Extension Service. *Bulbous Plants for Indoor Bloom.* Extension Bulletin 1021, College of Agriculture, Cornell University, Ithaca, New York.

North Carolina Agricultural Extension Service. *Forcing Bulbs Indoors.* Horticultural Information Leaflet No. 415, North Carolina State University, Raleigh, North Carolina.

BONSAI

U. S. Department of Agriculture. *Growing Bonsai.* Home and Garden Bulletin No. 206, Agusut 1973, Washington, D.C.

VEGETABLE GROWING

U. S. Department of Agriculture. *Minigardens for Vegetables.* Home and Garden Bulletin No. 163, May 1970, Washington, D.C.